Shetland's Heritage of Sail

Shetland's Heritage of Sail

Charlie Simpson

The Shetland Times Ltd.
Lerwick
2011

Shetland's Heritage of Sail

First published by The Shetland Times Ltd., 2011.

ISBN 978-1-904746-62-1

British Library Cataloguing-in-Publication Data
A catalogue record for this book is available from the British Library

Printed and published by
The Shetland Times Ltd.,
Gremista, Lerwick,
Shetland, Scotland. ZE1 0PX

CONTENTS

ILLUSTRATIONS

Principal sources of images:

Conway's History of the Ship: Conway Maritime Press 1995 – CHS
The Story of Sail: Veres Laszlo and Richard Woodman Chatham Publishing 1999 – SS
The Encyclopedia of Ships: ed. Tony Gibbons Silverdale Books Ltd. Leicester 2001 – ES

Chapter 1 – Inuit people in their kayaks – CHS
              Roman merchantman – CHS
              Oseberg Ship – CHS

Chapter 2 – Three Roskilde ships – CHS
              Saga Siglar plans – CHS
              Dim Riv – Keith Morrison

Chapter 3 – Bremen Cog – CHS
              Carrack of 1470 – SS

Chapter 4 – Dutch Fluits 1530ish – CHS
              English merchant ship c. 1550 – SS
              Early Dutch herring buss c. 1570 – CHS

Chapter 5 – Bleau's map – Self-published: James M. Irvine 2006; 11 Agates Lane, Ashtead,
                  Surrey KT21 2NG
              Buss of 1650 – ES

Chapter 6 – Dutch Speeljachts – *The Schooner*, David R. McGregor, Chatham Publishing 1997
              British naval cutter 1721 – ES
              Model of Dutch East Indiaman 1725 – CHS

Chapter 7 – Whalers around 1775 – *The British Whaling Trade*, Adam & Charles Black, 1978
              Mail packet – *Travellers in a Bygone Shetland*, Derek Flynn,
                  Scottish Academic Press Edinburgh 1989
              John Paul Jones at Lerwick – *Fred Irvine Pictures from Shetland's Past*,
                  The Shetland Times Ltd., 1969

FOREWORD

AS Shetland prepared for the return visit of the Tall Ships Races to Shetland in 2011 *The Shetland Times* published a series of articles by Charlie Simpson reminding us of our heritage of sail. It is a long and intricate story which, thankfully, Charlie has compressed into this short and easily read account, now published in book form.

'Sail' is the technology which determined the course of our islands' history. Anyone who has bent a car door on a breezy day will know it doesn't take much wit to recognise the power of the wind. Our ancestors used their ingenuity more wisely to harness windpower to their needs for there is only so much you can do with an oared vessel. To shift people or cargo over long distances or to access offshore fishing grounds sail was essential.

When Shetland's days of working sail ended away went the short rations, the hellish hard graft, the cold and wet, the days, months and even years away from family and friends and the ever-present risk of injury, ill-health and death. Seafaring under sail was too often a hard and brutish calling.

The Tall Ships Races, and Shetland's own restored sail-drifter, the *Swan*, introduce young people to a self-contained world where teamwork and self-reliance meld. If a few days on a modern sail training vessel is easy going compared to the lives of previous generations don't knock it. Technology may have sapped our strength and endurance and electronic aids dulled our instincts but nothing compares with the feel of a vessel under a press of canvas, or is more satisfying than seeing through the joys and tribulations of a passage completed under sail.

It is no insult to those whose livelihoods depended on sail to suggest that going to sea for the love of it is as noble a motivation as going to sea for the money or because there was, simply, no alternative. If nothing else it helps us understand the hardships our forebears faced and to appreciate more fully Shetland's heritage of sail.

Robert Wishart

PREFACE

IN the room where I write is an armchair of varnished pitch pine with curved armrests and turned legs, all fastened together with wooden pins instead of nails. It was made from the mast crutch of the sail drifter *Brothers Pride* by my grand-uncle John Bruce for my grandfather William Simpson, her skipper until her last herring season in 1936. My grandfather was in sail for all but three of the thirty-five herring seasons of his fishing career; John Bruce was the man who built the boat that carried him and four other Skaw men out to assist the American sailing ship *Marion Chilcott*, saving her from certain destruction in 1920.

The chair, and the *Pride*'s RNLI barometer on my kitchen wall, are constant reminders of the days of sail; of a time when a Shetland household without a seafarer was a rarity. I'm sure similar mementos still abound in homes all over the isles, but memories can fade and succeeding generations tend to know less of the deeds of their forebears. I've been interested in the subject all my life, so when Paul Riddell suggested a series of monthly articles for *The Shetland Times* as a run-up to the 2011 Tall Ships Race, it was a pleasant task to examine the story from beginning to end, and subsequently accede to the proposal that it be produced all under one cover in book form.

Most of the necessary reading was from books in preference to electronic media, and the rest from published sources including *New Shetlander* and *Shetland Life* – each a goldmine of historical tale and anecdote – and the superb resource that is Shetland Archives. My thanks are therefore due to all the staff in the library, the archives and the museum for their forebearance with my numerous requests for books, records and photographs; to Alex Dodge for the unavoidable internet searches, and to Joe Kay for the one elusive image the museum collection couldn't provide.

Because so many Shetlanders went to sea, there are so many stories; too many to include in a project of this scale. They're all in print somewhere, and my hope is that this little book will encourage others to delve deeper into this vast topic that ruled all Shetland life for so many centuries, and continues today albeit at a different level.

Introduction

THE first permanent settlers in Shetland arrived, we're told, some 5,500 years ago – and there are tantalising hints of earlier successful journeys. All had to come by sea, in boats; there was no other way. Indeed, every visitor to our isles, temporary or permanent, made the same voyage until 1918 when a military flying-boat first landed in Catfirth, a mere 93 years ago.

For 54 centuries at least then, the boat has been essential to the existence of every Shetlander, as the only means of arriving in the isles and the principal means of sustenance, once settled. It's generally accepted that sea-going craft assisted by sails were making voyages along the Mediterranean coast by 2000BC, and the rise of trade encouraged and spread the technology of hulls, keels, sails, seamanship and navigation at an accelerating pace around the coasts of Europe. By the time the Roman invaders crossed the English Channel there were decked ships capable of circumnavigating the British Isles and most, if not all, of the traffic between Shetland and the rest of Britain would have been sail-powered – while in Scandinavia the planked longships, capable eventually of crossing northern oceans, were steadily evolving.

Let's make a reasonable estimate, and assume 20 centuries of this kind of seafaring under sail to and from Shetland, or by Shetlanders. By contrast, it's a mere 18 decades since steam power liberated sea-going ships from the vagaries of the winds in the 1830s. Our heritage of sail is therefore far longer-lasting and more deeply embedded in us than most people resident in our isles today appreciate, where a seafaring career is an option pursued only by a minority. For most of our recorded history, seafaring was the occupation of the vast majority of Shetlanders, generally through necessity rather than choice.

I'm not going to pretend that this long era of sail was in any way a golden age – far from it. Throughout it, the sea took lives almost casually, and brought many to premature infirmity and incapacity through sheer toil. For the seaman under sail, discomfort, uncertainty, hardship, and danger, were never far away – more distant perhaps in the 21st century, but never completely absent. The acts of going and coming, exile and return, separation and reconciliation are central events in the seafarer's life, contrasting strongly with the settled existence of the landsman snug at home with his family ever-present.

And yet, there remain good points; positives from this era that endure today. There was the satisfaction of making a passage; of reaching a destination safely; the challenge for inventive minds to improve ships, sails and gear; to increase speed or carrying capacity, and to do it safely. Learning the work of a seaman or the arts of a navigator brought rewards. Knowledge was passed down to those who sought it – on the job, for it could not be gathered ashore.

Where human muscle power was the prime mover, the proper application of effort required teamwork; teamwork required harmony and leadership. To survive in his vocation a seaman had to possess intelligence at the outset, and to develop qualities including toughness, stamina, determination and patience. For survival ashore, his wife and family needed the same qualities – in almost equal measure. For centuries nearly every Shetland man went to sea for a living at some part of his life – mostly seasonally, it is true – and the people of the isles maintained these accumulated seafaring qualities and skills and knowledge through many generations.

Not every seaman is a fisherman, but every fisherman has to be a seaman. Through most of our peacetime history, Shetlanders going to sea in fishing craft have far outnumbered those in other seafaring activities. Although most fishing was prosecuted in small open boats relatively near to shore, the various fisheries were ideal training grounds for service in larger vessels when opportunities arose, and provided a valuable stepping stone for many a seafaring man to rise through the ranks and attain the highest heights of the profession.

Today, sail power in every commercial sense has long gone, yet admiration, veneration, respect – call it what you will – for the positives of life under canvas remain and flourish. Tall ships impress and excite even those with no idea of how or why sail works, for it's four or five generations ago since such knowledge was universal and a seafaring man in sail lived in most Shetland homes. With Lerwick a port of call for the 2011 Tall Ships Race, there's renewed interest in sail. This has prompted a look back over Shetland's heritage of sail to try to shed fresh light on the days of sailing ships and sailors and recount some of the innumerable tales from the era, especially for those who have not so far encountered them. Today, as I said, only a comparative handful of Shetlanders go to sea for a living, yet only a few generations ago there was a seafarer in every household. For all that, our links to the sea and seafaring are far closer and stronger than most of us realise.

Chapter 1

FROM PADDLES TO SAIL POWER

THE story begins long before sails were invented, in the time of the very earliest voyagers – those who ventured north first to explore, then to settle in our islands some 6,000 years ago. We must bear in mind that the human brain was as agile in Neolithic times as it is now, and banish any preconception that so-called 'Stone Age' man was less clever than his descendant of today. Innovative minds have created technical progress all through history, and one development led to another – especially after ores were mined and refined to produce metal in the Bronze and Iron Ages.

After those early immigrants, several thousand years passed before a sail was ever spotted on a Shetland horizon. It's obvious there are no tangible records of any kind to assist an understanding of what was essentially a very slow but inexorable march of technology, so we have to look sideways to identify documented advances elsewhere, and try to make these fit into a local chronology.

The earliest seagoing boats – capable of safe passage from Orkney to Shetland via Fair Isle – were almost certainly made of tanned animal skins stretched taut over a wooden frame, and propelled by paddle rather than oar or sail. The Inuit peoples in Arctic Canada and Greenland made perfectly seaworthy craft right up into the 19th century without using metal tools or fastenings, their boats ranging in size from the one-person kayak to the umiak capable of carrying a dozen people and half a tonne of cargo. All the raw materials for such boats were obtainable in Northern Europe – stone and bone for tools, trees and animals for timbers and hides.

Oars pivoting on a boat's gunwale were first noted in Egypt from around 4,500 years ago. Rowing is a much kinder process on the human frame than paddling; a given amount of muscular effort will take a boat much further, or for longer, than the same amount of energy expended with a paddle. Leather boats are flexible by their very nature, and hull coverings don't take kindly to friction, so oars rubbing against skin-clad gunwales or even wooden 'kabes' and 'rouths' pegged through holes in the skin could not be used. The paddle remained the favoured means of propelling skin boats for a long time; the Inuit probably saw Europeans using oars before adapting them. They solved the gunwale problem by sewing on extra sacrificial patches of hide where the oar slid, and instead of

1

The Inuit people of Arctic Canada and Greenland have been using kayaks for centuries.

kabe and routh as a fulcrum the rower simply pulled the oar against a length of lashing that secured the oar loosely to a wooden stringer inside the boat.

What of sails? Generally, to make a sail you need cloth of some kind; to make cloth you need a loom to weave yarn that has been spun. To set the sail you need wooden spars and strong cordage. It's known that there were seagoing craft in the Mediterranean with sails of cotton cloth 4,000 years ago, fair-weather craft most probably. These had an ancestry going back many, many millennia beginning with log rafts and reed-bundle boats, paddled then rowed, then sailed downstream in the Nile or the Tigris or the Euphrates. Agriculture had to develop widely before other fibres for cloth or cordage – flax and hemp for example – came into anything like widespread use.

Historians are very coy when it comes to discussing sails – even into Viking times; they tend to be more interested in hull construction and shape, building materials and techniques and so on. References to cordage and sailcloth are hard to find in the literature.

So, in our Shetland context, the paddle reigned supreme for thousands of years, possibly supplanted in due course by oar systems akin to those of the Inuit. During this span of time, metalworking and weaving arrived in Europe along with more organised systems of agriculture – and the beginnings of trade, the exchange of commodities between communities and individuals. Felsite axes and mace heads from Shetland were traded as far as England, around 3,500-4,000 years ago. Archaeological evidence of changing society over time, such as burial practice, is a clear indicator of fairly regular travel in and out of the isles.

2

Celtic peoples developed a sophisticated network of trade routes based on the navigable rivers of north western Europe, linked by pack-animal trails and augmented where feasible by sea voyages. The Greek merchant, Pytheas, described the export of Cornish tin into Gaul in 330BC; although he gave no details of the ships involved, the cross-Channel transport of tin ingots in any quantity needed robust seaworthy vessels, while sails of some kind would have been almost essential. The Celtic peoples of western Britain would surely have embraced this technology, so it's reasonable to assume that by roughly 2,200 years ago skin boats were being slowly replaced by planked wooden craft fastened together with iron nails. This is borne out by evidence in the form of coins and grave monuments of the period.

When the Romans resolved to invade Britain in 55BC, Julius Caesar recorded the naval struggle that ensued, and described the ships of the Veneti – the defending Celtic tribes inhabiting both sides of the Channel.

"The ships were built of oak and as such could cope with all sorts of weather… the traverse timbers were attached using iron nails as thick as a man's thumb… *For sails, the Veneti used hides and soft leather instead of linen…*"

Here, then, is an early clue regarding sails – the use of leather. In addition, these Veneti ships had a single mast and sail but no oars, so sail power had essentially come of age. Turning back to the technology of cloth, it's clear that Middle East cotton was the first fibre to be spun and woven, followed by flax in Roman times. The Roman invaders had 'linen' sails; obviously this cultivation had not yet reached more northern regions. Similarly, before hemp became available in these regions, there is record of cordage made from heather, plaited walrus hide, or lime bast (the fibrous inner bark of the lime tree).

A Roman merchantman prepares to moor, AD 50. A hand furls the sail by hauling on the brails while other hands go aloft to make the furled canvas secure.

3

In our Shetland context, we can postulate similar change in seafaring technology, albeit delayed by a few centuries as the new materials and ideas slowly percolated northward. So far, recorded voyaging of any kind is essentially 'coastal' – in sight of land all the time. The sea route to and from Shetland was via Fair Isle and Orkney, thence along either coast of Northern Britain. (It's true that a mariner leaving Fair Isle cannot see the north isles of Orkney, but there's an easy meid to give the correct course until Orkney land is sighted ahead.) The existence of our many brochs hints at seaborne strife as well as seaborne trade; if these structures are indeed defensive, their numbers and design suggest a serious threat by any account, and hint at events of increasing frequency.

To use a somewhat dated term, the Picts of Shetland would not have regarded a planked sailing ship as a novelty. As the brochs fell into ruin and decay, life went on; the ships came north and went south, to all intents and purposes peacefully. The papar, the holy men who brought Christianity to the isles were, of necessity, seafarers. Their leather boat technology took them north – and west to Faroe and beyond. To digress slightly a moment, it's interesting that the account of the famous *Brendan* voyage of 1978 from Ireland to Newfoundland devotes thousands of words to hull construction, but nothing whatsoever on sails of the period. *Brendan* was actually propelled by heavy duty Terylene.

Then, late in the eighth century AD, came the day that ships were seen on Shetland's eastern horizon carrying aggressors from unknown lands bent upon strife, upheaval of a terrifying kind and finally conquest; the Vikings had arrived.

Scandinavian boat technology followed a slightly different route to that of the Celtic peoples, its influences coming north through Germany and the Baltic regions, tempered by experiences there. Hulls constructed with planks overlapping were favoured, the planks sewn together at first and lashed to frames through cleats carved when the planks were split and shaped from tree trunks, then later nailed when iron nails became readily available.

The 'longship' was the favoured shape; by 100AD, oars had supplanted paddles, and the Danish Nydam boat of 310-320AD was fastened with iron nails. Sail took some time to become commonplace in Scandinavia; the longship excavated at Kvalsund, dating from 700AD, was purely a rowing boat. By 800AD, though, the Scandinavians had weaving looms capable of producing woollen twill which, when dressed with tallow and ochre, proved suitable for sailcloth. Clearly identifiable by its massive mast step, the oldest sailing boat so far found in Norway is the Oseberg ship, dating from around 815-820AD. It's therefore probable that the first Norse arrivals came in rowing boats, and that the first cloth sails would have come into use later by settlers and traders after the initial colonisation of the isles and the seeming extinction of the Pictish culture. Years of debate have blunted somewhat the notion of violent conquest followed by 'ethnic cleansing' for there is significant archaeological evidence favouring a peaceful assimilation of indigenous and immigrant culture – not least the indications that the settlers were farmers first and fishermen second.

The Oseberg ship, excavated and on display in the Viking Ship Museum in Bygdøy, dates from around 815-820AD.

Be that as it may, among the many skills and techniques brought to the isles by the Norsemen for the first time was the ability to navigate the open sea, out of sight of land for a significant period. I can't find specific mention in any of the saga literature or popular Viking histories to say which Norseman 'discovered' Shetland and when, only the story that the isles were used as a wintering base for Viking raids on the Norwegian coast, until King Harald Fine-Hair tired of their impudence, sailed west, and brought Orkney, Shetland, and the Hebrides under his rule. The discoverer of Shetland was probably not the first Viking to sail west, but he had to be the first to return east with the news. The early voyagers – sailing in the summer season with little darkness – used the sun by day and its afterglow by night, along with the Pole Star in early and late summer. Shetland lies almost due west from Bergen, but in poor visibility over several days a cumulative error of only 15° in the course made good would put a ship past Shetland without sight of land. Conversely, Norway is a virtually unmissable target when sailing east from Shetland.

The Norsemen also brought their boats with them, to give the isles a style of coastal and near-shore seafaring under sail that has endured to the present day – for more than 1,200 years.

Chapter 2

THE NORSEMEN AND THEIR TRADING VESSELS

THE first Norseman who discovered Shetland – and returned home with the news – is totally unknown, unnamed even in the tales of heroic and daring deeds that abound in the saga literature. It's a little sad he doesn't get a well deserved mention for he must have been a very talented seaman indeed. Evidence of archaeology and place names indicates that the earliest settlement could even predate the introduction of seagoing sails in coastal Norway, so it's quite possible the ship of discovery was rowed rather than sailed across the North Sea. It's recorded that population expansion and a shortage of suitably habitable land are the likeliest reasons for this movement west; I wonder how many adventurers missed our isles and voyaged into oblivion, before the first landfall was made? That said, my guess is that there had to be hints of the existence of this land west of Norway. More recent history gives us numerous examples of unfortunate Shetland individuals being blown away to Norway on a strong westerly wind, and surviving to tell the tale. This could have happened just as easily in Iron Age times – or later when holy men began voluntarily to voyage the northern oceans.

So, when this first ship from the east came – by accident or design – into some Shetland landing-place, what was the reaction of the inhabitants? Was there strife, or peaceful encounter? The first landing, at least, must have been peaceful; I doubt whether a crew that had rowed for 30 hours or more would be able to put up much of a fight against determined resistance onshore. Sadly, there are no answers on record.

Whatever the true story, its consequence was that the society and culture of the Norse colonists of Shetland soon became predominant in the isles, overwhelming almost totally that which had existed before, including language and place names. With settlement came possession and eventual political control in the hands of whoever held the Earldom of Orkney and Shetland, and a huge shift in the axis of Shetland's seaborne links. Islands that had been the dead end of a north-south route now became a cross-roads as Norse influence spread westwards to Faroe and Iceland, and southwards around Scotland as far as Dublin. From an islander's perspective, it's from this period onwards that sail becomes an integral part of local seafaring. Norsemen took many new things west to

Shetland besides their clinker-built iron-nailed boats – among them flocks of sheep, weaving looms, and the skills to make cloth.

Fragments of sail have been found along with the Gokstad and Oseberg ships, and all indications are that wool was the primary material for sailcloth for centuries before flaxen cloth came on the scene. Horsehair ropes were favoured for bolt-ropes and halyards, and the cloth was dressed with horse tallow. Sails thus created for replica Danish period vessels around 1980 proved to be effective enough, but vulnerable to damage in strong winds.

Woollen sails were in use in Iceland and Faroe right up to the 19th century, the threads spun on distaffs, the cloth woven on a warp-weighted loom such as the replica created at our Old Scatness site. The cloth produced was in panels around 600mm wide and up to five metres long, sewn together to make up the required area. When properly looked after, a sail would last from 30 to 50 years. In terms of labour, a sail was more expensive than the hull it propelled; a 16-metre seagoing replica trading ship took its Danish master builder and 10 men less than six months to build, while it took five people a whole year to weave enough cloth for its sail.

From 800 to 1000AD the Norse empire expanded and its societies began to take part in European trade and politics as nations, and it's during this period we see the evolution of two distinct ship types from a common ancestor. The cargo vessel for trading becomes more beamy and high-sided, heavily dependant on sail, while the warship stays slender and low, carrying armed men speedily under either sail or oars. Both types would have been a common sight in Shetland waters. There are saga stories aplenty of seaborne battles, sieges, punitive expeditions and plundering raids carrying on into the 13th century, when the fleet of Hakon Hakonson the Old was repelled by the Scots at the Battle of Largs in 1263. There are the voyages of discovery west to Faroe, Iceland, Greenland and America, many of them using Shetland as a stopping-off point on the way. There were shipwrecks, notably that of Earl Rognvald, builder of St Magnus Cathedral, whose ship was wrecked at Gulberwick when bound for the Holy Land. On an earlier visit, it's told how Rognvald went fishing in the Sumburgh roost with an old man whose crew had failed to turn up; he rowed the terrified fisherman right into the roost, then passed his share of the bumper catch to the poor.

The earliest Norse settlers in Shetland, we're told, were probably ordinary farmers. They grew grain, as the earlier islanders had done for several millennia. As the islands' population grew, however, there came a point in time – possibly even before the Norse settlement – when the farming technology of the period could not produce enough grain locally to feed everybody all year round. It's probable, therefore, that grain had to be imported in this early Norse period.

It's reasonable to assume that in these times fish stocks in the coastal waters round Shetland were, by modern standards, enormous, and fishing and boats soon featured prominently in the lives of the island farmers. Among the objects found at Jarlshof are iron boat nails and four drawings of boats or parts of boats, so it's highly likely that boatbuilding timber was another of the early commodities imported from the homeland. There was no need to go far offshore to fill one's boat, so it's unlikely that sails for small boats – the fourerns and sixerns – were used in fishing operations. Anyway, not everybody with a boat would have been able to afford such a labour- and resource-intensive commodity as a sail. As society became more ordered, there would have been visits to settlements to be made and taxes in kind to be collected by the king's representatives; goods such as wadmel cloth, butter and fish oil to be transported. Most probably then, a sail sighted around the Shetland coast meant power or authority of one kind or another, for a long time.

Eventually, though, trade – the exchange of commodities – evolved away from the movement of low-volume high-value goods such as tools, weapons, metalwork and glassware to include less valuable but bulkier goods like food products and building materials. To begin with, exchanges took place between producer and consumer, before the coming of the merchant middleman. In return for their grain and boat timber, the Shetlanders could offer dried fish in abundance.

There are no surviving documentary sources to tell us of these early trading developments between Shetland and Norway save for a brief mention from 1186, when, in Bergen, King Sverre welcomed traders coming from Orkney, Shetland, Faroe and Iceland. It's from this era that the fjord leading into Bergen from the north was named Hjeltefjord.

This development of trade was the driving force behind 1,000 years and more of improvements to the sailing ship in European waters. To begin with, though, seafaring in the first couple of centuries following the Norse settlement must have been a pretty uncertain business, even dangerous most of the time. Voyaging was a summertime activity, when the days were long and the weather benign in comparison with winter. Because such vessels and their rigs were pretty expensive to own, the 9th or 10th-century Shetland seagoing fleet numbered probably only a handful of craft, so the opportunity to sail in one would have been limited.

There were still fast, slender longships coming and going on voyages of discovery or conquest, while a heavier, beamier, deeper craft came into being for the safe carriage of people and goods. The 'knarr' was higher-sided than the longship, less easily rowed, more dependant upon its single square sail, but a sturdier and more weather-kindly craft. As we've seen, timber was probably the main import cargo, so it's obvious that the Shetland-owned knarrs would have been built in Norway. To imagine what a knarr looked like, think *Dim-Riv* (although Shetland's present-day galley might look warlike, in shape she's much more like the knarr). Readers may know of Ragnar Thorseth, the Norwegian adventurer who first rowed a fourern solo from Norway to Shetland in 1969. He returned to Shetland in 1989 aboard *Saga Siglar* – a replica of 'Ship No. 1' of the five craft discovered at Skuldelev, on Roskilde fjord in Denmark, in 1962. No. 1 was a broad and sturdy craft, 16.3 metres long and 4.5 metres in beam, contrasting sharply with No. 2, a longship of 29 metres but only around 4 metres wide. No. 1 had an open hold

Artist's impression of three different sizes of Roskilde ships.

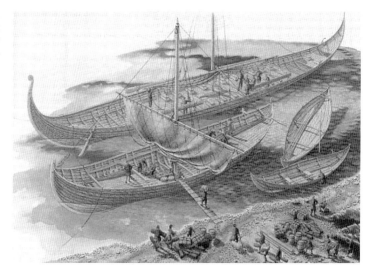

amidships that could probably load 20-25 tonnes of cargo, small decks fore and aft, and only a few oar holes in her sides.

Ragnar Thorseth had *Saga Siglar* built in Norway to test his contention that such a ship was capable of reaching Iceland and Greenland. In actual fact, he sailed his knarr replica right round the world via the Panama and Suez canals, making her the first ever open boat without a 'weather deck' to do so. She lasted until 1992 before finally foundering, without loss of life, in a terrible Mediterranean storm with winds in excess of 100mph.

That said, any ocean voyage in a typical ship of the early trading era was an adventure – and doubtless a pretty uncomfortable experience, wet and cold most of the time. The single square sail was most effective sailing before the wind, but not a lot of use when trying to make progress against the wind direction. Our mariners could wait for a favourable wind, of course; with generally westerly or south-westerly winds prevailing in our regions, a fair wind for the passage from Shetland eastwards could be anticipated with some confidence. On the other hand, the fair wind necessary for a good return passage – from any easterly direction – was less predictable, so there must have been many a long wait in the fjords for the wind to favour the ship's safe return home.

The ships were essentially open, making stowage and care of the cargo a perpetual challenge during every voyage, especially when carrying produce such as dried fish or grain that needed to be kept away from rain, spray or bilge-water. Shelter for the crew was temporary and scanty for there was no watertight deck to rest or sleep under. On coasting voyages it might be possible to anchor in a sheltered harbour each night, perhaps even cooking and sleeping ashore, but on a sea passage there was no such luxury. Open cooking fires in an open boat simply don't work; while our haaf sixerns of the

9

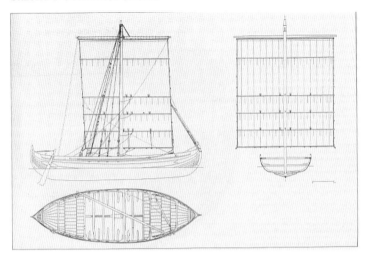

The plans of *Saga Siglar*.

19th century had a 'fire kettle', this piece of kit could do little more than boil water for tea – which of course was unknown in Europe of the first millennium. Any food such as meat or fish had to be pre-cooked, and the drink taken cold – a choice of water, blaand or possibly beer. Modern replicas have the luxury of gas cookers, and *Saga Siglar* had a low enclosed cabin built amidships to give her crew respite from the elements. The original had no such refinement, and while waterproof and windproof garments for modern yachtsmen are efficient and affordable, in the Middle Ages there was only wool and skin.

In our latitudes it's always appreciably colder at sea than on land, and the retention of body heat is essential. Today we have synthetic materials; waterproof cloth, rubber boots, fleecy garments. As recently as my grandfathers' early lifetime there were none of these. Seaboots were of leather, heavily greased; oilskins were exactly that – coats or 'smookies' made from cotton or serge liberally and repeatedly coated with linseed oil – fish or seal oil in earlier times. Multiple layers of woollen garments from the skin outwards provided the insulation. It's recorded that sheepskin waistcoats, worn with the skin side out, were commonly used by 19th-century Shetland fishermen.

* * *

I wrote earlier that Norway was unmissable from Shetland; keep travelling east and you can't fail to reach it. The real trick was to reach one's intended destination port or harbour safely without getting wrecked on some unknown skerry or outlying island. In the days before the magnetic compass came into general use it wasn't too difficult for a seasoned mariner to shape a course due east using the sun. He could discern direction from the bearings of sunrise and sunset, and observe the sun's greatest height in the sky to give both time of day and a bearing of due south.

Naturally, winds and tides affect the course made good across the sea, as distinct from the course steered. This inevitable unknown error made landfall the crucial part of the whole voyage, for the shape of the land – especially the mountain peaks of west Norway – was the clue to the ship's whereabouts on the coast, and a vital indicator of the course to be followed into harbour. In this context the idea of a pilot – someone who had been before – was nearly essential (I was once told by a Shetland Bus man from Norway that every crew that set out on a mission from Shetland had a man aboard familiar with the land around the place their ship was heading for).

However, steering the correct course and gaining the intended landfall were both dependent on good visibility. With the sun out of sight and visibility reduced by rain, low cloud or fog, the navigator lost his ability to stay on course, for the wind direction could not be relied on for very long. In these circumstances, a North Sea crossing could become a nightmare for the navigator – in either direction. He could only hope to avoid land until the visibility improved, and then to guess successfully which way his ship had wandered over the ocean in the meantime. The sagas often relate that after a period of misty weather seamen would lose their bearings; they went into a state known as

Shetland's own Viking ship, the *Dim Riv*.

'hafvilla' – 'sea delusion'. In view of the potential hazards, the rewards for a successful return voyage must have been high.

Such was the state of seafaring throughout 500 years or so – most of the Norse period of Shetland's history. By the end of the 11th century, the knarr design had improved until it could sail fairly well to windward; and Scandinavian waters were seeing different designs of ships coming from further south in Europe – the Baltic shores and the Low Countries – ships created to make sea transport and trading easier, safer, quicker, or cheaper; all in the cause of profit, it must be said. Innovations aboard these craft included a rudder hung from the sternpost, followed by a bowsprit and bowlines to keep the leading edge of the sail tight when beating to windward. In the 13th century came further advances; the magnetic compass, sailcloth of flax and cordage of hemp, then truly decked craft with dry shelter for crews.

Norway and its satellites supplied northern Europe with dried fish, in return for grain. Grain supplies from growing production in Baltic lands ousted imports from England, and a new influx of traders arrived in west Norway from towns in north Germany. Operating in small groups called 'hanser', their activities were later to unite cities in mercantile cooperation, becoming known eventually as the Hanseatic League. This organisation was to dominate trade in northern Europe for the next 500 years – and indirectly produce very fundamental innovation in seafaring technology. The era of the 'ship merchants' in Shetland was approaching.

Chapter 3

DEVELOPING TRADE WITH THE HANSEATIC LEAGUE

AFTER five centuries of Norse domination and occupation in Shetland, new influences in the 14th century slowly brought change to society and the old patterns of sea trade to and from the islands. From a seafaring perspective Shetland was still a maritime crossroads where many sea routes intersected, although the major voyages of discovery or conquest were long in the past. Norway to Faroe, Iceland and westward; Norway to Orkney, the Western Isles and southward; Norway to Scotland: bound hither, private ships of all kinds passed regularly through Shetland on their various missions, while royal or earldom longships still came and went. The domain of the Norwegian kings had contracted as first Dublin, then the Isle of Man and the Hebrides, shook off the Norse yoke: in this context, worse was yet to come.

Whatever deep-sea opportunities came the way of adventurous young Shetlanders we can only guess at, although it's safe to infer that these were pretty limited, and most island seafarers simply got on with their fishing, drawing cod from the coastal waters' teeming abundance to dry and send to Bergen in Shetland-based knarrs. The seagoing ships of Shetland were still essentially open clinker-built craft, only marginally different from those used to occupy the islands, and they probably sailed on well into the 15th century.

Farther south, though, improvement in ship design, rig and operation began early in the 13th century – for example, the invention around 1200 of the stern-hung rudder, superior to the steering oar. Ultimately, these improvements created vessels able to keep the sea for weeks, and voyage directly to Shetland from far-flung foreign ports.

Expanding seaborne trade drove these changes, as safer and more efficient means of transporting goods and commodities were demanded and developed. The Baltic regions, in addition to their food grain crops, were now producing flax and hemp in quantity for the production of sailcloth and cordage. Fine flax yarn wove into linen; the coarser yarns were turned into canvas – first recorded in 1260 – stronger, heavier and less stretchy than woollen cloth. Hemp ropes did not swell when wet, and so were ideal for running rigging – ropes that led through sheaves and pulley blocks.

The new generation of cargo-carrying ships in the Low Countries and Baltic regions were built flat in the bottom, broad in the beam and high in the side for greater capacity, with straighter, steeper stems in contrast to the sweeping curves of the Scandinavian vessels. Stout crossbeams, originally incorporated into hulls to give added strength, were floored over to make a deck above an enclosed hold for cargo. These early holds were not weather-tight, for the crossbeams passed out through the hull sides and were notched over the planks to give stiffness to the structure. These vessels were called 'cogs' – very different from the double-ended open boats of Scandinavia.

The cog was still clinker-built, but with a tool new to the region – the saw – hull planking no longer had to be split from logs. A split plank in width could only equal the radius of the log, whereas a sawn plank – a slice – could be twice as wide. The reduction in the number of planks required meant fewer seams to fasten, fewer nails, and so on; cogs were quicker and cheaper to build than their forerunners. To keep their deep hulls free of water, bilge pumps were introduced in place of the simple bailing bucket, for the cog was still essentially an 'open' boat in that the decking was not watertight. Much cargo thus had to be transported in barrels, to keep it dry in transit.

Following close behind these Baltic developments, ship designers of the coastal regions west of the Rhine estuary used the same clinker-building technology to improve on the cog concept and produce a ship with its top strakes sweeping up at the ends – almost like the planks of a modern Lerwick Up-Helly-A' galley. This ship type was known as a 'hulk', a more efficient sailer and cargo-carrier than the cog, and it soon found general favour with ship-owners everywhere. Cogs and hulks revolutionised sea transport in Northern Europe, moving larger quantities of foodstuffs, textiles and more valuable cargo, expanding trade in all directions.

The 'hanse' model of trading originated in north German seaports and the number of hanse towns, cities and ports grew until their loose organisation of mutual self-interests was recognised Europe-wide as the Hanseatic League. Hanse loosely translates as band or flock; a hanse was a group of men with ships and capital, plus the acquired knowledge and skills to travel and trade, sharing the risks and the profits.

Initially, Shetland was unaffected by this process and the islands' direct trade with Norway continued. As the League slowly spread its activities northwards, however, its members had a growing influence on Norway's internal trade. Bergen was the main centre of distribution for dried fish from northern Norway, Orkney, Shetland, Iceland and Faroe; gradually the aggressive merchants from south gained complete domination in the entire trade by the 1340s. Naturally the hanse merchants in Bergen's Bryggen sought to extend their own activities to Norway's regions – eliminating the Norwegian middlemen – and it was simply the challenge of reaching Shetland that took them so long to get here.

It's unlikely a cog ever sailed over a Shetland horizon, for the type was best suited to coastal voyaging, its flat bottom and bluff shape making it an indifferent sailer to windward or in the swells of the open ocean. Cogs could and did make the challenging passage from the Baltic to Bergen, north through the Danish sounds and west around the south

Reconstruction of Bremen cog wreck discovered in 1962.

end of Norway, but a sheltered haven was never far away along this essentially coastal route. Gradually the hulk type of ship, with its superior construction and performance, ousted the cog from common use as shipwrights responded to the demands of trade to turn out bigger craft, more efficient, more seaworthy, and more profitable. Although the single-masted, square-sailed, clinker-built carrier faded from general usage, it didn't die out completely, for Hebridean galleys were used well into the 17th century while the jekts of coastal Norway sailed on into the 20th century.

In times of war, the cog and the hulk became warships in the sense that they were used to carry soldiers for an invasion. Before the days of gunpowder, sea fights merely involved an archery contest between rival craft, and occasional boarding with hand-to-hand combat. Temporary 'castles' rigged up at the ends of the ships to give commanding height for the launch of missiles eventually became permanent with their sides boarded in to create shelters for crew; the officers in the 'aftercastle' and the sailors, less comfortably, in the smaller 'forecastle'.

In the 15th century, a new type of construction originating from the Mediterranean found rapid favour in northern waters, as the 'carrack' and the 'caravel' ousted the hulk and the cog. These craft were 'carvel-built' in contrast to the clinker hull whose planks were shaped and fastened into a shell before the internal frames were fitted. A carvel builder began by erecting the frames on the keel to create a skeleton for the hull, which was then covered with planking, laid edge to edge instead of overlapping. This process gave a stronger, more rigid hull than the earlier vessels and did away with beams notched through planking. A carvel-built ship's decks were close-planked and caulked to give, for the first time in a ship of Northern Europe, a watertight hull able to carry dry cargo more satisfactorily. A further benefit – from the crew's viewpoint – was the hugely enhanced habitability of the vessel.

Carrack of 1470.

Up to this point in time trading voyages in the region had been essentially a business of the summer months of longer daylight and better weather; now, for the ship-owner or trader, the enhanced seaworthiness of the new designs brought the prospect of a longer sailing season – and voyages involving much greater distances than hitherto. By the first decades of the 15th century, foreign traders seeking to obtain Shetland's products at source were sailing regularly to the islands, cutting out the Norway-based participants of the trading triangle altogether, although their route from home still took them north past Denmark, around the Norwegian coast to Bergen, then west to Shetland. In effect, the newcomers brought to Shetland the trade goods that Shetlanders previously had to fetch from Norway – simply moving the point of transaction westwards.

These traders were from Hamburg or Bremen; men still maintaining independence from the rules and edicts of the Hanseatic League. They came in the aftermath of the Black Death, the great bubonic plague epidemic that arrived in Europe from Asia in 1348, reaching Shetland and Norway in 1349. It's reckoned that upwards of a third of Europe's population died, and the subsequent social upheavals and economic depression took decades to stabilise. Norway, itself, came under the domination of Denmark; there was weakness both in Norwegian government and the Bergen Office of the Hanseatic League – and the new traders took advantage.

In addition, it was around this time that the magnetic compass came into general use by mariners. Up to then, just about the only tool of the navigator was the lead-line for sounding the depth of water. Voyage information for passages between ports was recorded in 'pilot books', while sun and stars were the only means of steering a proper course out of sight of land. The compass gave assurance to the mariner in poor visibility or darkness, and provided the confidence to undertake protracted open-sea passages. The scene was set for an influx of ships into Shetland waters – not only from the east, but from Scottish and English ports besides.

A most momentous event in Shetland's seafaring history took place in 1415 when, it's recorded, the first trading vessel arrived in Shetland after sailing directly from Hamburg. This voyage is noteworthy because its success depended upon the bringing together of crucial developments in hull and sail design and construction, navigation tools and theories, together with improvements in the habitability of ships that allowed long voyages to be endured by seafarers. What manner of vessel, then, came to anchor in some Shetland haven – the Pool of Virkie or Symbister perhaps – her crew keener than any previous arrival to stretch legs ashore, imbibe cool spring water or taste meat free of brine?

We can make reasonably accurate guesses in this respect, for the rapid rate of 14th-century improvement in maritime technology slowed comparatively to a snail's pace, more or less until the coming of the Industrial Revolution in the 18th century. If you could transport a 1415 sailor forwards in time and land him aboard a trading ship of 1815, he would manage his job fairly easily; although the ship might be larger and the rig a little more complex, the fundamental principles of building and sailing ships were practically unchanged over 400 years and more.

Imagine if you can a vessel built of wood, twice the length and width of Shetland's *Dim-Riv* and maybe four times deeper from keel to main deck; her bow bluff, her stern above the waterline square across, with upper deck structures at bow and stern to accommodate her crew. This early 15th-century craft probably had one mast amidships with one large square sail, although two or even three masts were a possibility. She would certainly have sported a bowsprit, developed to extend and tension the luff or fore edge of the sail to improve the sailing performance to windward. As craft became larger and longer it was found that a sail, set on a spar hung below this bowsprit or on a 'fore' mast, improved sailing performance even further – but only if it was balanced by a third sail set on another mast placed aft – so it's possible our ship was so rigged. The sails were of woven flax canvas and the rigging of hemp rope. The rudder was hung from the sternpost, worked by a long helm because the steering wheel had not yet been invented. Forward hung an iron anchor, its massive hempen cable stored below and led out through a hawsehole. On deck were a windlass with a horizontal barrel for working the anchor, and a capstan with a vertical barrel for hoisting sails and working cargo. Both were powered by men pulling or pushing on short poles fitting into sockets on the barrels. To keep the bilges dry there was a pump – a vertical tube inside which a shaft, with pistons fitted with valves, could slide up and down. Bilge water was carried up the tube and overboard with each stroke of the human-powered pump handle.

Below decks there were bulkheads (vertical partitions to divide the hull into compartments for ease of stowing everything carried on board) and perhaps even platforms – half-decks – at each end of the hull. For the crew there were water barrels and stores of food, along with a galley, as the cooking space became known. Cooking by fire aboard a wooden ship was a hazardous business, and safety had to be paramount. Fire risk was minimised by placing the fire in contrivances such as a sand-filled iron cauldron, or a brick-lined hearth inside an iron box, on deck initially, but moved below decks as innovations minimised the risks. Because tea and coffee were yet to be discovered in 15th-century Europe, beer became the favourite drink onboard, not least because it kept drinkable far longer than plain water stored in a wooden cask. It's probable that the cook's skills needed to rise no further than boiling salt meat – or pea soup, perhaps. The crew found shelter from the elements in the built-up spaces fore and aft, the officers always with more space and in more comfort than the sailors. The same held good in another respect, for the officers usually had a wooden lavatory seat fitted somewhere about the stern overhang while the men had to make do out in the open over either side of the bow.

By the early 1400s, the Shetland fisheries were a thoroughly commercial operation. Shetland dried ling and cod had a good reputation for quality and were well received in the market. The ship merchants came in May as the summer fishing began, and based themselves where fishing effort was concentrated, for example in Cullivoe, Symbister, Grutness and Skeld. Initially they traded by barter, later introducing cash into the transactions. They sought the produce of the country – dried fish predominantly, but fish oil, butter and possibly woollen cloth or knitted goods. They gave in return "hooks and lines for the taking of cod and ling, Nets for the taking of herring, Brandie and strong waters of all sorts; Mead, strong beer, Bisket, Wheat-Meal and Rye-Meal, Barley and Salt"; and in later years "Tobacco, Fruits of all Sorts, Monmouth caps and the Coarser Sort of Cloth and Linen, and such like merchandise". The fish acquired were cured by salting, drying, or a combination of both. At the end of the season in late August, the ship, hopefully empty of trade goods, was loaded with island produce for the return voyage to Germany.

The ship merchants carried on this practice for almost three centuries, occupying numerous anchorages every season, some building or hiring booths and stores onshore, some even staying ashore for the winter. Their vessels' visits became routine all around the isles, and it's from this era onwards you could say that all Shetlanders became really familiar with sea-going ships.

There was some competition right from the start of this ship merchant era. English and Dutch vessels began to come north every season to fish for themselves, and were always ready to trade a little at the same time. Later in the century, Denmark fell out with the Hanseatic League, becoming embroiled in conflicts that weakened both financially and led to the pledging of Orkney and Shetland to Scotland in 1469. A consequence of this action was the eventual immigration of a class of Scots landowners that began to change Shetland's socio-economic structures and slowly but surely – over several centuries – shifted the focus of seaborne trade and intercourse away from Norway and northern Europe, in favour of Scotland. It's also from this period onwards that the published record plays an increasingly prominent part in the story.

Chapter 4

PIRACY AND POLITICS

AS sailing craft developed and grew in size, more power – in the form of sail area – was needed to move them. This, along with the need to keep the propelling forces safely in balance when sailing to windward, led to the evolution of the three-masted ship.

This process began back in the longship days, when it was found that bowlines – ropes fixed to keep the leading edge of the sail taut – helped the windward performance. Bowlines were secured to the ship's stem at first, but worked even better when they were led further forward from a boom extending beyond the stem. Thus came into being the bowsprit; later, some inventive mariner hung a little square sail from a yard attached to it, and found that his ship could point up even higher into the wind. If the sail was too big, however, the balance of forces could be altered and the performance suffered. One remedy was to fit a sail on a second mast near the stern of the ship to restore the balance, and make the ship sail better again. In the 15th century, a foremast was often added to carry another forward sail, in addition to the bowsprit sail. Thus evolved foremast, mainmast and mizzenmast with single square sails; eventually the masts could set two or even three smaller and more manageable sails each. In early designs the mizzen was derived from Mediterranean practice, a triangular 'lateen' sail set from a long, steeply canted yard.

Merchant vessel design was always driven by the need for financial efficiency; bigger and faster ships on one hand, more economical to operate on the other. While a three-master might cost more than a single-master to build and rig, over her lifetime she would carry much more cargo on many more voyages, with fewer crew. The Low Countries led the way in this respect, evolving the 'fluit', a vessel type capable of easy adaption to various trades and widely copied by shipbuilders all round the North Sea. In Spain and Portugal, the three-masted square-rigger gained in favour over the lateen rigs.

These improvements to European ships led to exploration of the oceans, followed by increased seaborne trade as new lands and resources were discovered. Portuguese mariners led the way by sailing south and west, at first down the coast of Africa in the 1430s until Bartholomew Diaz finally rounded the Cape of Good Hope in 1487. Christopher Columbus sailed from Spain to America in 1492 while, in 1497, John Cabot took a more

Dutch fluits from around 1530.

Bartholomew Diaz.

John Cabot.

northerly route to Newfoundland. On his way home to Bristol, Cabot sailed across the Grand Banks, where his crew caught huge quantities of cod merely by lowering baskets into the sea. The Dutch and English ventured northward, seeking to reach China and the Indies over the top of the world. By the mid-15th century Dutch, English, and Scottish fishermen were regularly fishing in Shetland waters.

Back in Shetland, the inhabitants learnt in 1469 that their king, Christian I of Denmark, had mortgaged his rights and lands in the islands to King James III of Scotland. A year later, the last Sinclair Earl of Orkney renounced his title and, in 1472, the Scottish parliament formally annexed the earldom of Orkney and the lordship of Shetland to the crown. By 1485, Sir David Sinclair, natural son of the last Earl, was a leading figure in Shetland. We find the first recorded

21

King James III of Scotland.

mention of a Shetland-owned ship in his will of 1506: "... To my Lorde Sincler I giewe and leiffis... my schipe callit the Carvell wyth her pertinentis..."

There were political rumblings, local power struggles and disputes over landholdings between Shetlanders, Orcadians and Norwegians, but from a seafaring and trading perspective, change came only gradually. The merchant ships sailed in and out every season as before, although east across the water the controlling influences of the hanse and the Norwegian authorities over the traders slowly waned, so that the direct trade from German ports to Shetland increased at the expense of the Bergen-centred trade.

While maritime incidents and details of sea trade begin to crop up in the legal records of the period, there is hardly any technical detail about the ships involved. We know that around the start of the 16th century the typical Hanseatic trading ship was small, from 60 to 80 tons only, with five to 18 men in its crew; a vessel of the caravel type, her hull fully decked and flush-planked over a framework. The name of Sir David Sinclair's ship – *Carvell* – is an indicator that she was probably of the same type.

With bigger ships able to make longer voyages, the 16th century was a time of increasing maritime activity in Shetland waters as passing visitors sought to exploit new opportunities. A significant new discovery came in 1553 when the English captain, Richard Chancellor, on an expedition of three ships seeking a north-east passage to India, sailed round the North Cape of Norway and through the White Sea to Archangel, thus opening the northern trade route to Russia.

The Norway trade still endured, although erratically as early records show. In 1519 only one Shetland ship visited Bergen, and in 1521, out of 108 foreign ships loading there, only two were from the isles. By 1566-7, however, customs records from Sunnhordland, south of Bergen, show seven Shetland ships loading cargoes of timber and boats – a trade that was to endure for almost three centuries. A special kind of boat's spar – mast

English merchant
ship of about 1550.

or yard – was known as a 'hjeltespirer'; in one year, 700 of them went to Shetland. In the year from May 1577 to May 1578, four small Shetland ships loaded timber and boats in Sunnhordland. These are described as "small vessels; three pinks of 17 lasts and a yacht of 16 lasts". A last was 4,000lbs, or nearly two tonnes – a measure of weight rather than

Early Dutch
herring buss, circa
1570.

volume. A 'pink' was any small square-rigged ship with a square overhanging stern, while 'yacht' is probably a mistranslation of the Norwegian 'jekt', the single-masted derivation of the knarr of Viking times. Interestingly, the word yacht only came into the English language when Charles II was presented with a Dutch pleasure craft – the original 'royal yacht'.

A prominent figure in this trade was Andrew Mouat of Ollaberry, who is recorded as merchant and shipmaster travelling regularly to Norway with fish, returning with timber products. His second wife was Norwegian, from the Sunnhordland area, and he settled there. With more seaborne visitors to Shetland, life and trade had its risks: in 1586, Mouat's house in Ollaberry was plundered by Englishmen led by Alexander Chapman, captain of the ship *Black Lion* of Hull. Later, in 1590, having almost completed a voyage from Norway, Mouat's ship was boarded by an "Inglishe man of ware" and relieved of money and goods to the value of 4,500 rix-dollars.

The change in Shetland's governance gained momentum in the latter part of the 16th century, especially after 1565 when Queen Mary granted her lands in Orkney and Shetland to her half-brother, Robert Stewart. While he wasn't by any means the first Scot to seek power or possessions in the North Isles – or to bend laws for personal gain – his rule, and that of his son Patrick Stewart, coincided with an increase in maritime conflict and lawlessness as notable as their deeds and misdeeds on land.

Even before Robert Stewart's arrival in the isles there was strife, for piracy was becoming a way of life in northern waters. A complaint by four German traders to the Council and Senate of Bremen, concerning events in Shetland in 1566, gives us a graphic picture.

Hermann Schroder stated that when he came to Shetland on 28th May with his own and his friends' ship and goods to the accustomed port of Quailsundis (Symbister), there were two ships called busses fitted out for piracy, which were soon followed by others. He was unexpectedly attacked

Mary Queen of Scots.

by James Edmistoun, captain; George Foggo, skipper; William Simessen, quartermaster; John Blacader, George Blak and their accomplices. "I was overcome by armed force, our ship and the booths that we have there were wretchedly pillaged, bronze cannons and all the provisions there taken away, casks of merchandise and chests smashed and all their contents plundered... they carried off our beer, imported meal, iron and canvas... they violently removed my wallet with gold and silver from my person... In the end we were not even left with what was needed to work the ship, for they took away our new anchor and cordage... with difficulty we returned at length safe and sound to our native land..."

Three days later, the same gang arrived in Uyeasound and subjected the merchants there to similar treatment. Segeband Detken and Johannes Beking lost 24 tuns of meal and 12 tuns of beer, along with all the goods in their booth plus cordage and sails. In early June, the pirates ambushed and robbed Theodoric Fogen in Symbister and Joannes Michael in Cullivoe. The first victims, Detken and Beking, were ambushed for a second time in the port of Hammeltonge (possibly Hamnavoe, Yell) by another gang of Orcadian and Scots pirates. In July, this gang assailed Humerius Meiger at night, attacking and plundering his ship and booth in Scalloway. Justice finally caught up with some of the pirates in Edinburgh, for Edmistoun was beheaded and Blacader hanged for piracy in September the following year.

There was more strife of a different kind in 1567, and again an innocent German merchant was to suffer loss in a momentous year for Scotland. In February, Queen Mary's husband, Henry Darnley, was murdered, the first of many violent events that led to her downfall. In May she married James Hepburn, Earl of Bothwell, precipitating civil war; by mid-June she was a prisoner of the rebels and Bothwell, declared outlaw, had fled. In July Mary was forced to abdicate in favour of her infant son, crowned James VI of Scotland five days later.

Bothwell, created Duke of Orkney and Shetland by Mary, fled first to Orkney. Finding no succour there he carried on northwards, pursued by an expedition led by Sir William Kirkcaldy of Grange and William Murray of Tullibardine, joined in Orkney by Adam Bothwell, bishop of Orkney.

Gerdt Hemelingk, trader and merchant of Bremen, was loading his season's cargo of salt fish aboard his ship *Pelican* in a Shetland harbour entitled 'upt Ness' in 'Swineborchovet' – probably the Pool of Virkie – when Bothwell arrived there in mid-August with men and ships.

The Scotsman and the German later gave conflicting accounts of how it happened, but when the *Pelican* sailed from her Ness harbour soon after, her owner and cargo had been dumped on land and the ship was now part of Bothwell's little fleet, bound for Bressay Sound. On the morning of 25th August, Bothwell was ashore with his "captains and men of war" when Kirkcaldy's four warships entered the harbour at daybreak, doubtless causing consternation. The masters of Bothwell's ships cut anchor cables, set sail and headed out the North Mouth, hotly pursued.

Bothwell escaped capture that day, and a Shetland baa off the mouth of Dales Voe received its immortal name, for Kirkcaldy's flagship *Unicorn*, leading the pursuit, hit the baa and soon sank. The fugitives got clean away in the confusion while the men of the *Unicorn* were being rescued. Bothwell rejoined his fleet in Unst and vanished eastward toward Norway, leaving his pursuers to return home to the Forth. Gerdt Hemelingk never saw his *Pelican* again. Bothwell was arrested in Norway and died insane in a Danish prison in 1578. Mary, his widow, lost her head in 1587. Only the 'Unicorn' remains today, its position marked by a buoy for all to see.

Robert Stewart came north to his islands, and maritime misdeeds continued. In May 1574, he and his men boarded two English merchant and fishing vessels off Shetland. The *Michael* and the *Mynioun* were taken to Scalloway, their crews charged with spurious crimes, and the ships stripped of cargoes and ordnance. If English ships were fair game, German ones were not, for in June the same year Robert condemned five Shetlanders for plundering a ship from Emden while it was sheltering off Nesting. They took cloth, money, sails and rigging before casting the vessel adrift, never to be seen more.

On the other hand, Robert had legitimate authority to suppress piracy – when it suited him – for in 1579 he was commanded by King James VI to seek out a Captain Clerk, leader of a crew of "divers pyrattis and utheris brokin men" whose ship frequented Shetland harbours while preying upon Danish vessels.

Clerk was not alone; piracy was rife in the late 16th century and continued into the next, as Robert's star waned and his son Patrick came to power in the isles. The year 1588 was, of course, notable for the defeat of the Spanish Armada's attack on England and the trail of Spanish shipwrecks and tribulations around the north and west coasts of Great Britain in the autumn, as the battered ships sought to return to Spain. From a Shetland perspective, the main event was the wreck of the store-ship *El Gran Grifon* on Fair Isle. The ship had wallowed to-and-fro for nearly five weeks in autumn gales, and was in a sinking condition when she grounded at Stroms Hellier on 27th September. Nearly 300 soldiers and crew, exhausted and malnourished, managed to reach dry land by climbing the masts that lay against the cliffs before the ship broke up. There were 17 households on the island, so there was scant shelter for so many, let alone sustenance; the weather even prevented the Fair Isle men from catching fish in any quantity. It was 27th October before a boat could set out for Shetland with news of the island's plight, and 14th November before a ship arrived, by which time 50 of the shipwrecked men had died of hunger. This vessel, belonging to Andrew Umphray of Berry in Scalloway, is interesting in that she was large enough to take aboard all of the 250 Spaniards still alive. She carried them via Quendale to Anstruther; eventually they reached home – after a year spent in Leith.

By 1592 Patrick Stewart was well entrenched in the northern isles, styling himself "Erle of Orknay, Lord Yetland and Justice generall of the samin". He himself had been a victim of piracy in 1590; on a trip from Orkney to attend court in Edinburgh his ship was attacked by English pirates and all his worldly goods plundered. Perhaps this is why, by all accounts, he was described as a rapacious character, never content with the considerable legitimate income he derived from the northern isles, always seeking enrichment by fair means or foul, on both land and sea. No chance of gain or profit was missed, it seems; in 1592 he plundered the *Noah's Ark* of Danzig after the ship had been run ashore in a storm. He legitimately bought another wreck in 1594, the Dutch merchant ship *Flieing Hairt*, ashore on Burra Isle. Even the possibility of gain from the wreck of the *El Gran Grifon* attracted him, for in 1593 he funded one William Irving of Sabay in Orkney to salvage and "win ye ordinance that was in the Spangyirt scheep", in return for two-thirds of any profit realised.

For Shetland the 16th century came to a close with piracy and strife at sea adding to the normal risks faced by seafarers and fishermen, while on land their Stewart overlord took what he could from them. By this era ships of significant size were operating from Shetland, owned by prominent men such as Andrew Umphray and Andrew Mouat; in the absence of any record we can only suppose that their crews were Shetlanders. The early years of the next century heralded more change as Earl Patrick's deeds led to his demise and execution in 1615. By then, fleets of ships from the Netherlands were heading for northern waters every summer, and a handful of these were bound even further north in search of prey of a different kind. The herring fishers had arrived – and the whalers would eventually follow.

Chapter 5

Dutchmen, Herring and Strife

AT the start of the 17th century, Shetland's fleet of deep-sea ships was small, its owners mostly men of substance. The vessels were of contemporary design, able to make long voyages out of sight of land, and were more than ever the essential link between Shetland and the outside world, including European ports far away from the old routes to Orkney or Norway. The open knarrs had become an outmoded rarity in most deep-sea trades, but the new craft maintained the timeless pattern of commerce, carrying away the exports upon which the prosperity of the islands depended, and bringing back the necessaries the inhabitants could not produce for themselves. For their owners the ships could also be a means of communication to sympathetic ears in Scotland when the grasping control of the Stewart earls became intolerable. Despite the ongoing improvements to ships and seafaring, deep-sea voyaging was still an activity for the summer season; contact with Shetland was curtailed every autumn, leaving the islands virtually inaccessible in wintertime.

Early maps of the British Isles existed in the 1580s and more detailed maps of Orkney and Shetland were published in Amsterdam in 1636 and 1654. Compass courses and distances between ports were now slightly better known, but navigation was still a matter of 'dead reckoning'. The navigator had to keep careful estimate of the courses and distances actually sailed as the ship made her way towards her destination, plotting the ship's estimated position regularly, and applying corrections to the ship's compass course in order to keep on track. Needless to say, this was at best a fairly haphazard process assisted only by the magnetic compass and the sounding line, although the quadrant, an early astronomical measuring instrument, had been perfected by Sir John Davis in the late 1580s and very slowly came into general use for mariners . Nevertheless, 17th-century seafaring was such an ordinary activity for Shetlanders involved in it that very little is on record even in legal documents, save occasional episodes of piracy, shipwrecks, cargo contracts or rare ship sale agreements.

About the ships and the sailors we can only guess. We know that the earls were ship-owners; the first mariner mentioned in a document is Andrew Allan – from Kirkwall originally – who was master of Earl Patrick's ship *Thomas* in 1587. By 1606, he was

**Blaeu's map of
Shetland, circa
1654.**

sailing out of Scalloway in command of his master's *Dunkirk*. Patrick also owned
the *Rainbow*, bought new from Crail in Fife, in 1598. Laurence Sinclair of Gott and
James Leslie of Braewick bought their ship, *Lyoun*, in 1598 from Robert Williamson of
Dysart in Fife. In 1601, when Hew Sinclair of Burra and Petir Johnesoun in Cuppaster
exchanged a piece of land, the deed of excambion was witnessed by "Arthour and
Thomas Quhytis, mariners" – probably the first identification of native Shetland sailors.
We have already met ship-owners Andrew Mouat of Ollaberry and Andrew Umphray
of Burra in the previous chapter; in 1611, Umphray owned a ship called the *Fortoun*,
carrying fish to Newcastle. When Robert Sinclair died in 1616, he owned a ship "valued
at £2,000 Scots".

The German ship merchants dominated onshore trade, although English and Scots traders were now regular visitors. The Norway trade continued, mainly in timber and boats; from 1597 to 1627, around 12 ships came from Shetland each year in ballast, mainly to ports in Sunnhordland, south of Bergen. Records show around 20 boats taken back each year – fourerns mainly, with sixerns increasingly towards the end of the century. In 1633 it was written of the inhabitants of Unst that "they usually have a bark that they trade with to Norway, where they may buy timber for houses ready framed, deal boards, tar, ships, barks and boats of all sorts, and other necessaries for their use".

By now, English fishermen were regularly venturing as far north as Iceland for cod and ling, but to the Scots fishing was still a near-shore activity, dependent upon curing and drying the catch on land. Lord Robert Stewart made agreements with Scots fishermen regarding shore facilities in Dunrossness during his period of power, and Earl Patrick renewed these contracts. Fishermen from Crail, Pittenweem and Anstruther were permitted to fish, build houses and stores for drying and packing their catches, and buy necessaries from the local inhabitants. Well over 100 vessels were involved – 30 at Ronas Voe and 90 at the Ness. In 1604, the Fife men brought 37 brewers to keep the fleet supplied with beer and ale and, in 1613, their fleet was joined by 18 doggers from Fisherrow, with their "cost syde men" – the curers who worked ashore. For all that, British fishing effort around Shetland was puny by comparison with the scale of Dutch operations, developed over almost a century until 500 vessels fished herring in Shetland waters each season.

Before the northern part became an independent state, leaving the southern part under Spanish rule through various dynastic unions among European royal families, the Netherlands in the 15th century were ruled by of the Dukes of Burgundy. Between Burgundy and France there was permanent rivalry and strife, short of open warfare. Fish was a universally important food, and the French did their best to hamper the coastal fisheries of Flanders, Zeeland and Holland. This, along with an interruption in the supply of Baltic herring imports, increased demand for fish and led to the development by the Dutch of 'deep-sea' fishing, out in the North Sea far away from their own coastal waters, catching herring by drift-nets and salt-curing the catch on board ship. By 1482, the vessel employed – the herring 'buss' – was a craft capable of voyaging to fish with safety and ease north in Shetland waters.

The buss first appeared in documents of 1405 and became the backbone of the region's herring fishing industry for nearly 500 years. Besides accommodation for a fair-sized crew, it had deck space to work drift nets and room below for barrels and salt. The carvel-built hull was broad, deep and squarish in section, bluff at the bow and square at the stern. Compared with earlier hull forms it combined large cargo space and long length. Busses were three-masted, each with one square sail. During fishing operations the two forward masts were lowered to rest on a frame, leaving the mizzen sail to keep the ship drifting head to wind while the nets were in the water. Most busses were of around 100 tons and 25 metres in length. The ton in this context is a measure of volume rather than weight, originally the amount of space needed to stow a tun of wine – a barrel holding 216 gallons.

By 1469, the first Dutch busses were fishing the Shetland herring grounds in summer, initially from July as a precursor to the fisheries off the Scottish coast and off East Anglia later in the season. The idea of a starting date for the fishery came about because of French aggression, for Dutch busses were organised in fleets and escorted by warships throughout the voyage. The buss was an adaptable craft, equally effective as a cargo ship, and its basic features were soon imitated right round the coasts of the North Sea – bluff capacious hull, three masts, a simple rig of square sails. The design was scaled up a little and became known as the 'fluit' in the Low Countries and the 'flyboat' in England. Scaled down it was known as the 'dogger', used primarily for line fishing. Into the 16th century just about every sailing ship seen in Shetland waters was modelled on one or the other. The Hanseatic traders owned them; English fishermen sailed them up as far as Iceland to trade or to fish; Scots ventured all round the North Sea in them.

There is a perception that Dutch busses came in their thousands, but modern sources put the maximum number at around 500 busses, plus escort vessels and 'vent-jagers' (wind-hunters) – the fast ships employed to carry cured herring back to Holland in advance of the fishing fleet. Busses gathered in Bressay Sound towards midsummer in preparation

A buss of 1650.

for fishing operations which began on St John's Day, 24th June, and returned at intervals to tranship their cured fish into the vent-jagers. Probably every Shetlander was well aware of the fleet's presence – and the marketing opportunities afforded for local produce of various kinds. Authority frowned upon the unlicensed trading that went on, for the booths erected on the west shores of the sound were ordered to be demolished in 1615. Gradually, the traders crept back until, in 1625, the Sheriff-principal in Scalloway "being informit of the great abominatioun and wickedness committit yeirlie be the Hollenderis, and cuntrie people, godless and prophane persones, repairing to thame at the housis of Lerwick... committing manifold adultrie and furnicatioun with women venteris of beir and utheris women evill inclyned quha resortis thither under pretext of selling of sokis and utheris necessaris to thame... ordains the said housis to be utterlie dimolished and down cassin to the ground be the haill awneris thereof..." In addition, the women of Shetland "of quhatsumever rank or qualitie" were banned from going to Lerwick to sell "sockis", but were allowed to send their "husbandis, sones or servandis" into this den of iniquity instead. Trading also took place at the Hollanders' Knowe in Gulberwick, and at Levenwick. Woollen stockings and fresh foodstuffs were exchanged for tobacco, brandy, leather footwear and, most importantly, money. The Sheriff's prohibitions were soon ignored; Lerwick, as we know, has continued to expand for nearly five centuries.

The busses tried to make three trips every fishing season. The first was to Shetland for matties and full herring; the second to the middle waters of the North Sea, around St James' Day on 25th July; and finally a trip to the East Anglian coast, between the time of the feast of St Bartholomew on 25th August and that of St Martin on 11th November. The early voyage was normally the most successful, and it is reckoned that up to 40 per cent of all herring sold out of Amsterdam was caught in Shetland waters. The salt herring were exported all over Europe. The wealth from all the Dutch herring trade funded colonial expansion and a swift rise of Dutch influence in the maritime world, the effects of which were experienced in Shetland for a very long time.

* * *

The island of Spitsbergen, and its whale stocks, were discovered in 1586 by Dutchman Willem Barentz, unsuccessfully seeking a northern route to India over the pole; and again in 1608 by Englishman Henry Hudson, unsuccessfully seeking a north-east passage to India. When English whalers of the Muscovy Company reached Spitsbergen they found the Dutch firmly in control of the best harbours and whaling areas – and a 50-year struggle for supremacy began. Both copied the ancient methods of Basque whalers, killing whales near shore and boiling the blubber on land, so harbours were vital.

Whale oil was used mainly in soap making. The Dutch did consistently better than their rivals, controlling and dominating the European oil market; at the peak of effort, it's said that 18,000 men worked ashore on Spitsbergen every season. In the end, the English effort petered out in bankruptcy around 1684, while nearly 200 Dutch ships still went successfully north. When whales became scarce round Spitsbergen, the Dutch sought and found new stocks down the east coast of Greenland, which they exploited with bigger ships that simply brought the raw blubber back to port in casks for processing ashore. Dutch exploration in more temperate zones of the globe led to the establishment of colonies in the East and West Indies and trade boomed, especially after the founding of the Dutch East India Company in 1602.

A great deal of the shipping involved in these Dutch activities had contact with Shetland in one way or another throughout the 17th century, in addition to the herring fleet. The Dutch were almost perpetually at odds with Spain and France, so in wartime most outward bound ships in the Dutch colonial trade had to be escorted through the English Channel by warships, while a few sailed north around the British Isles. Homeward bound Indiamen did the same, making a rendezvous with waiting warship escorts usually near Fair Isle or Unst, before passing down the North Sea in convoy. This practice continued one way or another for nearly 200 years, as did the fishery. Dutch craft of all kinds passing, calling – or being wrecked – were a completely familiar sight in Shetland waters.

News of any kind took a long time to reach Shetland in 17th-century Europe. The continent was perpetually beset by the religious and dynastic squabbles of rulers, the political quirks and turns of governments, and the resulting wars and rebellions within and between states. Ordinary Shetlanders heard nothing of these events, so as the century unfolded it must have been confusing, to say the least, to learn who was at war with whom – or whether a visiting ship came with peaceful intent or otherwise. The Stewart king, James VI of Scotland, became King James I of England in 1603, which to a degree sorted out conflicts between Scots and English fishermen. The wealthy Dutch built a navy to protect their maritime interests from the Spanish, the French and frequently the English.

This prompted enlargement of the British navy in turn – significantly for Shetland in years to come – for, in 1631, the impressment of seamen for naval service was put permanently on the statute book of King Charles I. In June 1640, three armed Dutch East Indiamen and a warship, anchored in Bressay Sound, were set upon by a fleet of ten Spanish; in the one-sided action that followed the warship surrendered, *De Haan* and *De Reiger* were burnt and sunk on Lerwick's shore, while the fleeing *De Jonas* only got as far as Gletness before meeting the same fate. The remains of *De Haan* were dredged up in 1922, just north of Alexandra Wharf; among the recoveries were four iron cannon, one of which now stands beside the lower entrance of the Shetland Hotel in Holmsgarth Road.

Civil war in England between king and parliament broke out in 1642; Charles I lost his head in 1649. The Commonwealth government went to war with the Dutch in 1652 – and only a storm prevented a major sea battle off Shetland. An English fleet of 60 ships under Blake sailed north from the Thames to harry Dutch shipping, and by the time it reached Shetland waters it had captured 12 ships and sunk many more, taking 900 prisoners. Blake was pursued north by a Dutch fleet of 96 ships under Admiral

Tromp, hurrying to protect the returning fleet of Dutch Indiamen. Between Fair Isle and Shetland the two fleets sighted each other, but a south-westerly storm arose, leaving Tromp's fleet struggling west of Shetland to keep away from a deadly lee shore, while Blake sought shelter along the east coast. Many of Tromp's ships found shelter, notably 23 at Scalloway, but two were wrecked and two sunk at sea. When the weather eased both fleets headed for home, Blake very short of stores and anxious to hang on to his prizes and prisoners.

The throne of England was restored in 1660 and occupied by Charles II, but rivalry with the Dutch continued. Another English fleet of 100 sail under Montagu visited Bressay Sound in 1665, along with a party of engineers and soldiers sent to build a fort to defend the growing community of Lerwick and its strategic harbour. Although many Dutch Indiamen had taken refuge in Bergen, Montagu eventually captured 45 of them before he returned to the Thames. Maintaining the sea traffic to the Indies was such an absolute priority for the Dutch that in 1667 they sent a fleet of 24 sail to protect returning Indiamen – and capture Shetland in the process. Off Noss they were told that an English fleet was in the vicinity, and that the fort in Lerwick had 1,000 men and 40 guns. None of this was strictly true but the stratagems worked and the Dutch gave up the idea of conquest – temporarily as it turned out. Seven years later, in 1673, the countries went to war for the third time and the Dutch acted quickly before the Lerwick fort was rearmed and garrisoned. A landing party came ashore with little or no resistance and burnt the fort along with many of the houses in Lerwick. For the rest of the 1600s any warfare in Shetland waters was between Holland and France; each seeking to protect its own sea trade while disrupting that of its enemy.

Shetland mariners were mostly spectators to these martial events although a few were temporarily kidnapped for information now and then. Wrecks were probably of more interest, with the opportunities for material gain they represented. It's said of the wreck of the Dutch East Indiaman *Kennemerlandt* on Skerries in 1664 that the news only leaked out when a boat from Whalsay, sent to discover why the Skerries men hadn't come to buy their Yule dram, found the whole adult community had been drunk for many days on the vast quantity of good spirits saved from the wreck.

The Shetland fisheries had changed little over the 17th century, although the use of long-lines by the Dutch and English had been noted and would be imitated. Hitherto most fishing was done in two-man fourerns with handlines within "two or three leagues" of the shore, but that was about to change, for the 'Little Ice Age' was under way, causing fish to move offshore, while there was famine and epidemic on land. Wars with the Dutch had underlined the need for a strong navy, and steps were afoot to encourage the creation of a big pool of seafarers upon which to draw for naval manpower in the future. Fishing effort would increase – and the British whaling industry would rise again. More sinisterly, the permanent impressment laws gave the Royal Navy sweeping powers to take seamen almost at will. Shetland would share in the benefits of the former, and suffer the pain of the latter, as the 18th century came along.

Chapter 6

THE END OF DUTCH SUPREMACY

WE have already seen how the Dutch had been at the forefront of ship design and rig for several centuries. Their innovations continued into the 17th century, first with the 'speeljachts' created for the wealthiest burgomasters of Amsterdam – craft built purely for the pleasure of sailing rather than any martial or commercial purpose. Some were two-masters with only two sails, each set with a short gaff at the peak and a boom at the foot, both spars secured to the mast at one end only, and able to swing from side to side. The boom was controlled and adjusted by a rope known as a 'sheet' and, depending on the course chosen, the driving force of the wind could be directed to either side of the sail with equal effect. This was an enormous advance in efficiency; before this innovation, the sails of 'square-rigged' vessels were designed to operate with the wind astern – only on one side of the sail. When trying to make good a course to windward, square-riggers could point little higher than 70° to the wind direction, whereas it was found that a fore-and-aft rigged vessel could point 50° to the wind. Head to wind, a square-rigger was effectively forced backwards, whereas with a fore-and-aft rig there was no driving force and the sails simply flapped, as flags do. Soon after, the triangular jib – a sail set on the fore rigging stay that supported the foremast – came into widespread use, and made the performance to windward even better. The new rig was quickly adopted on both sides of the Atlantic and ships so fitted eventually became known as schooners. Although larger schooners commonly set a couple of square topsails to aid down-wind performance, the pure fore-and-aft rig performed well, as already described. The sails were hoisted and handled entirely from deck level, could be easily reefed as the wind increased, and needed far fewer crew. It became virtually universal for small ships, and its variants – the cutter, the ketch, and the smack – are the most popular sailing rigs even to this day.

Looking seaward throughout the 17th century, a Shetlander could have been forgiven for thinking the ocean all around belonged to the Dutch Republic, such was its maritime influence in fisheries, whaling, colonial trade – and the energetic protection of these interests through its naval forces. Despite all this energy and innovation the Dutch had rivals at every turn, whose gaining strength was slowly but surely to erode Dutch supremacy over the next 100 years.

Early fore and aft sail – Dutch speeljacht of the 17th century.

The last decades of the century were for Europe a time of wars, famine, disease and climate change – the period of the 'Little Ice Age'. In Shetland, a succession of poor harvests caused great hardship and the fisheries declined when fish moved further offshore. Many estates went bankrupt because tenants could not pay rent. The estate of Brew in Dunrossness was obliterated by blowing sand; the Pool of Virkie silted up. Although Britain was not involved in a Dutch-French war, there was a great deal of French privateering activity in northern waters against Dutch merchant ships and whalers. They harried the German ship merchants too; men already with troubles of their own, for growing British government regulation of their activities was slowly bringing their

Shetland trading to an end. Shetland suffered widespread depredations ashore from the French who landed to seek water, fuel and provisions. There was practically no defence against such raids, and the French sailors more or less helped themselves to whatever they needed. The story is told of an Unst lass, hailed a heroine for strangling a plundering Frenchman with the neck-band of the kishie which he had wrenched from her and slung over his shoulder. To cap it all, the first of several severe epidemics of smallpox took many lives in 1700.

A fresh European war began in 1701, with Dutch and British allied for once against a resurgent France in a conflict that had disastrous consequences for the Dutch herring fishery. In June 1703, four French warships attacked the escorts of a large fleet of Dutch busses off Fair Isle. At the end of a heated defensive action, the protecting Dutch frigate, *Wolfswinkel*, was blown up by her commander in preference to surrender, whereupon her consorts retreated and the busses fled for Bressay Sound. The French caught up with them there and set fire to over 150 defenceless busses, only sparing as many as were needed to carry home the stranded crews. Many fishermen were killed; those who lost their ships were beggared, and the Dutch herring industry never completely recovered.

In 1711, the Earl of Morton petitioned Queen Anne – fruitlessly – to have Lerwick's fort repaired and garrisoned: "… Several French privateers were on that coast who within two months past burned three ships and taken five others in Brasey Sound, and came on shore, carried off the people, cattle and other provisions for victualling their privateers…" At least the importance of Lerwick as a port was recognised, along with the revenue-raising opportunities that arose, for a Customs House was established there in 1712. The war lasted until 1714.

The offshore movement of fish stocks had huge repercussions for the Shetland economy, for fewer fish to catch meant less dried fish for export and less revenue in rents and dues for landowners. British governments had for long been envious of the success of foreign fishing activities in British waters, and had regularly sought to protect national interests in fisheries and trade by means of various Navigation Acts favouring British shipping at the expense of foreign vessels, coupled with taxes on salt for fish-curing. After the parliamentary union between Scotland and England in 1707, these acts were enforced with new energy. There was no immediate effect on foreign fisheries but the German ship merchants fell victim to the laws. Finally forced out, they came to Shetland no more after 1710.

In modern parlance, there was a severe economic downturn, and a vacuum where the German traders had fitted into the Shetland economy. Shetlanders needed fish hooks, cordage, salt, shoes, candles, soap, tobacco, spirits, meal and lots more; no longer were these essentials and luxuries readily available every summer from the booths and ships of the Hamburg, Lubeck or Bremen merchants. It took years of effort to restore the fisheries, strengthen exports to afford imports again, and establish a fleet of trading ships for the purpose. This was mainly achieved by a small number of landowners who had avoided the recession of the 1690s; notably Gifford of Busta, Henderson of Gardie, Mitchell of Girlsta, and Nicolson of Lochend. They were instrumental in forging the classic landlord-tenant relationship with its obligation on the tenant to fish and sell his catch to his landlord. Hitherto, most fishing had been prosecuted only a few miles offshore; now that the fish stocks were to be found ten miles or more from land, better boats were sought, and the sixern gradually began to predominate in the 1740s.

The Norway trade in boats continued. A 1714 report states that the boats exported from Godoysund, near Bergen, were "... only clinked together with a few nails and before being taken on board the ship they are numbered and marked and then taken apart again and when the ships arrive at their place of destination, they are discharged and put together in accordance with the afore-mentioned numbers and marks; thus a small ship's hold can carry 80, 100 or even 120 boats". In a list of imports from Bergen of 1731 is included "6 pises hemp linin for boats sails" – the first definite evidence that oars were no longer the sole propulsion method in small boats.

British naval cutter of 1721.

For the ordinary Shetlander the change in fishing methods meant that new seafaring skills had to be perfected, to safely exploit the offshore fish stocks during the summer season when the weather was most settled. Ling was the predominant catch, far ahead of cod, while inshore, saithe caught in the roosts were significant in weight but much less in value. In 1727, the Government began to pay a bounty on fish caught and cured. This measure was part of a century-long quest by governments, jealous of the Dutch dominance of North Sea fisheries, seeking to encourage expansion of the national fishing production. Fishery companies had regularly been floated and just as regularly failed, usually through inefficiency, or corruption, or plain ignorance. The bounty helped to expand the Shetland boat fishery, despite a massive increase in English and French cod-fishing production from Newfoundland that depressed prices. Demand for ling remained reasonable nevertheless, and new curing methods adopted in the 1730s helped to open up new markets, especially in Spain. John Gifford of Busta wrote to his father, Thomas, in 1738 "… if you please to make a Tryall of four or five hundred Ling and Cure them after the new method, that is just fresh out of the sea, Right Spekded [cleaned], prest, Little Salted, and hard dryed… it be fact that fish thus cured will give far better price at any market". Beaches suitable for laying out fish to dry assumed a new value, and those nearest the prolific deep-water fishing grounds also became valuable 'home ports' for boats and their crews during the season. The classic pattern of the 'far haaf' and its centres of activity – Fethaland, Stenness, Gloup, Funzie, Skerries – was emerging.

The new breed of laird-merchants needed vessels of their own, to carry away the exports and bring back the essentials. Most of them were known as 'sloops' – not really a type of rig but a name derived from the French 'chaloup' meaning any kind of small sailing vessel, generally fore-and-aft rigged. They were little ships, easy to handle in and out of Shetland's voes; probably small enough to be beached on an autumn spring tide and hauled up snug over the winter, for before the 1730s Shetland was entirely bereft of any kind of jetty or pier where a ship could float alongside. A mainly triangular trading pattern emerged; the sloops would load dried fish, butter or fish oil locally, deliver this export cargo to Hamburg, sail to the Bergen area, take on boats or timber, and return home. Sometimes the route was Shetland-Leith-Hamburg, while the foreign port might be Danzig or Gothenburg. Thomas Gifford of Busta, in a letter of January 1731 to a Leith merchant, wrote somewhat scathingly of his shipmaster "… Alexr. Picarne who set out for Gothenburg, but was put in again and lyes here yet being affrayed to go ther for the frost, but will set out nixt month for that place, from thence to Leith… when he is discharged at Leith, you may order him to Goasund in Norway, wher he is to load timber for Zetland…"

Essential goods for fishermen and luxuries for merchants might be carried back from either foreign port, as the following commission from Thomas Gifford to his agent in Hamburg records, in July 1730, ordering "20 barles 60 ankers corne brandie for the fishers, three half hogsheads french brandie, 24 barles fishing lines, 'most ground lines', 10 thousand ling hooks, 24000 haddock hooks, 2 half barles starch, 4 firkins soap, 12 barles tarr, 1 fall good mum [possibly a barrel of wheat beer], 1 anker [8 ½ gallons] best sherry, 1 do Frontignac, 2 ankers new french wine, 1 anker best white port wine or Lisbon, ½ anker vinegar, 30 lb raisins, 30 do. Proons, 20 lb faigs, 6 lb almonds, 6 lb peper, 4 lb whyte ginger, 12lb hunney, 20 lb currents, 30 lb ryce, ½ lb nutmegs, ½ mace, ½ cinamon, ¼ lb cloves, 4 lb confected ginger, 12 lbs best Hollands broun mustard, 12 papers pins, 12 bolts whyte tape, 1lb course, ¼ lb fine sowing whyte thread, 12lb hair powder, 2 bottles florence oyll, 1 barle of barlie, 2 barlls flour, 1 barrell biscuit, ½ barrell pease, 6 lb azer [blue dye], 2lb table indigo, 2lb rock indigoe, 3 last [about 6 tons] Spanish salt – or what she may need for ballast in bulk, and pipstaves [cask staves] to make her full. All to be shipped in the 'St. Andrew', Wm. Mason master, for my account and risque of Thomas Gifford."

'Risques' there were aplenty, for the *St Andrew* was wrecked on Quendale sands on 29th September, 1731. As technology produced better ships and gear, there was temptation to keep voyaging for more of the year, especially in autumn in order to export the products of the summer season. As days shortened, the weather became less settled and the risks grew, especially as there was still no reliable method of knowing one's longitude, while the use of instruments to observe latitude from sun or stars was general, especially after the invention of the sextant in 1731. The multitude of hazards all round the rock-bound coasts of the northern isles were generally known only to local mariners, and such a thing as a lighthouse would be unknown for another century at

Model of Dutch East Indiaman of 1725.

least. Even local knowledge was of little avail in darkness, and in fierce winds and heavy seas very few sailing craft were stout enough to make windward progress against such elements and sail clear of a threatening lee shore. It's little wonder, then, that wrecks were commonplace, especially in the dark days of early spring and late autumn. The cliffs and skerries of Shetland took a terrible toll of Dutch whalers, both inward and outward bound, along with many Dutch, Swedish and Danish East Indiamen, generally outward bound, while locally owned ships were always at risk, at home or abroad. To the Shetlander, while life was saved from the sea wherever possible, wreckage or wreck goods were a godsend, often to the exasperation of local ministers. 1744, in particular, was a bad year for Swedish ships. In September the out-bound East Indiaman, *Stockholm*, wrecked north of Troswick in Dunrossness on a foggy hairst morning; her crew of 24 landed safely, but after only the 'moveables' and some cargo had been salvaged the ship broke up in a gale. Wine and spirits in casks were saved intact, assuring many in the parish of a jolly time. Only twelve weeks later, the folks of Lerwick were next to benefit when another Swedish East Indiaman, the *Sveriges Drottning*, wrecked herself on the South Ness at Twageos. It's said her wreck was plundered of "many casks of spirits". Later, in 1745, her bell was presented to the Kirk Session of Lerwick; it hung in the kirk until 1782 when it was recast.

* * *

Not every trading vessel belonged to a merchant laird, for the records show sloops owned by men who were first-and-foremost mariners carrying cargoes for others. George Mouat of Stenness was owner and master of the sloop *Concord*, of 25 tons, built at Leith in 1733. With Thomas Gifford's nephew, John, aboard to look after his uncle's interests, she loaded Gifford's herring and salt ling in Hillswick and sailed on 3rd July, 1736, for Hamburg, the cargo consigned to Hendrick Scholle, merchant there. The orders were to take on "4 or 5 gret lasts" of salt for ballast, along with tobacco and sailcloth, then to proceed to Bergen for boats. *Concord* delivered her cargo safely to Hamburg and sailed for Bergen in August.

With her cargo of boats loaded she cleared the coast of Norway for home, but faced a succession of gales. After a long struggle, she entered St Magnus Bay and came within two miles of Hillswick, but as darkness fell a northerly gale came up, a sail blew out, and Mouat had to bear away before the wind for the shelter of Swarbacks Minn. In the darkness, the entrance channel between Muckle Roe and Vementry couldn't be seen so the ship was brought to anchor with her best bower and 60 fathoms of cable. As the wind increased another anchor was dropped; both dragged until the unfortunate *Concord* eventually grounded on the back of Vementry and sank. John Gifford, Mouat, and the crew – mate William Farquhar, sailors William McKindly, Henry Halcrow and Thomas Keith – got ashore safely but all the cargo was lost. Thomas Gifford bought the wreck, raised and repaired her, and sent the *Concord* back to sea with McKindly as master.

Mouat, left greatly in debt to Gifford and others, abandoned creditors, wife and family to seek better fortune in Virginia.

Thomas Gifford employed the *Concord* on several more voyages to Hamburg and Leith but she finally came to grief in a heavy gale, in October 1739; in command of the same nephew, John Gifford, she was bound home from Hamburg to Hillswick – late in the season – and foundered with all hands off Sumburgh. Fragments of ship and cargo washed ashore at Troswick were the only evidence of tragedy, which took the lives of her master, his brother Andrew, Robert Clark, John Anderson, Alexander Corner, Andrew Laurenson and Robert Simon Halcrow, the ship's boy. Also lost were passengers James Peterson of Scalloway and James Hunter, brother of the laird of Lunna.

The lee shore consumed ships remorselessly, as at Symbister in 1748 when the topsail schooner, *William and Robert*, loaded with dried salt fish for Hamburg, had to be run ashore after she began to fill with water when anchored off Saltness in a hurricane from west-south-west. The crew were saved, the cargo all lost, and the wreck – "not worth repairing" – was sold for £19. On the same day, the *Belsher*, a Scottish ship with a cargo of "zetland goods" was wrecked on Turra Taing in the north entrance to Lerwick harbour. For many decades afterwards, the taing was known as 'Belcher's Point', while her master, John Bourmeister, who settled in Lerwick, was later pressed into the Royal Navy and ended his days as an Admiral.

Such was life – or the ending of it – for Shetland sailors in the early part of the 18th century. As the merchant lairds gained trading experience more innovations were in the offing; notably for the future a Spanish market for dried ling was opening, while an early attempt by Arthur Nicolson of Lochend to fish cod with his sloop, in 1744, was stymied when she was assailed and plundered by a French privateer. The British government was becoming more aware of the need to create and maintain a pool of trained seamen to man the navy in time of war, so moves were afoot to award tonnage bounties – subsidies – to ship-owners in the fishing and whaling industries.

Despite its dismal beginning and what would now be called a severe recession, the first half of the 18th century for Shetland was a period of slow but significant maritime and trade expansion. It set the scene for seafaring vocations that were to endure for a century or more, involve most of the male population of the isles, and transform Shetlanders from 'subsistence farmers with boats' to 'fishermen and seamen with crofts'. By the century's end, more or less every Shetland male had experience of sail, in the haaf fishery, the Greenland whale fishery, the merchant service, or – less willingly – the Royal Navy.

Chapter 7

TO THE GREENLAND WHALING ... AND TO WAR

BEFORE 1700, few Shetlanders served in seagoing ships, for only a dozen vessels or so, mostly belonging to the main landowners, were then in commission. Voyaging was a seasonal summertime business normally, with the ships laid up snug in voe heads in winter. There was hardly any full-time employment for wages, apart perhaps from a few lairds' retainers and ministers. You could say that for most Shetlanders the need to subsist gave them perpetual self-employment; from the land they produced crops and animals while the sea provided more fish than they could eat. Spare butter, fish oil and dried fish paid their taxes and rents in kind, and were bartered for imported essentials. While monetary value was an essential part of this barter process, cash – coin of the realm – was hardly needed and thus a rarity before the coming of Dutch fishermen who paid money for their stockings and cabbages, bringing coin into local circulation and introducing notions of monetary gain and hoarded wealth.

Sailors were probably paid in kind at the end of each voyaging season too, as were the hundreds of fishermen who ventured offshore in open boats to catch fish to cure for the export trade. Instead of money, a man earned credit with a merchant – usually his laird – who supplied the meal and tobacco and tea, the shoe leather, linen and thread and all the other contemporary 'essentials' he and his family could not produce for themselves.

While this simplistic model took nearly two centuries to fade away, the early part of the 18th century saw the start of a transition to a money- and wage-based economy. Opportunities arose for Shetland men to gain paid employment as the advance of British technology from the 1740s onwards – the Industrial Revolution – created new demands and produced increasingly effective systems and means to satisfy them. The multitude of skills learnt in open boats made the home fishery an ideal training ground to qualify a man for work aboard a merchant trader or a whaler, and when the opportunities offered, young Shetlanders were quick to accept.

A big event after 1750 was the rebirth of the British whaling industry, eclipsed earlier by the Dutch until only three English whale-ships operated in the 1730s. The government, ever keen to create and maintain a significant pool of seafarers to man ships of the Royal Navy in time of war, increased annual bounties payable to owners of fishing boats and whaling ships. Over the century the bounty varied between 20/- and 50/- per ton, subject to various conditions. With these bounty payments and a rising demand for whale oil, the British whaling fleet grew from three ships to 83 in less than a decade.

Interestingly, it was actually illegal to employ Shetlanders in the bounty era, for one condition of payment was that all the whale-ship's crew had to be aboard at her home port when the voyage began. Relaxed only in 1793 when war started, its observation was largely ignored; over 50 whaling ships a year visited Shetland from 1755 onwards taking on hundreds of men especially for their skills in handling small boats. Every man signing on a Greenland whaler meant one potential fisherman lost to the home fishing; many lairds took a dim view of this and there are tales of whaling men being fined a sovereign for going away, and of their families sometimes threatened with eviction.

The whaling ships arrived in March, anchoring in Bressay Sound for up to a week to recruit men and top up with water and provisions for the coming voyage. By this time, whaling had become pelagic in the sense that a shore base for flensing and boiling the whale oil out of the blubber was no longer needed. The ships worked along the edge of the pack ice on the east coast of Greenland, or up the Davis Straits on the west coast, able to stay at sea for five or six months without replenishment. Whales were harpooned from open rowing boats, crewed by six oarsmen and a boat-steerer.

The Greenland right whale, so-called because it was the 'right' species to hunt, was a slow-moving toothless creature that fed on shrimps by filtering them through a fringe of baleen plates hung from its upper jaw. It was usually oblivious to a stealthily approaching whaleboat, until the first harpoon was thrown or physically forced into its body by the harpooner, whereupon it would dive, often taking out all 1,400 metres of line carried in the boat. A whaling ship carried from four to six boats usually; when the whale came up again this whole fleet would be waiting, to stab the whale with long lances until it bled to death. Towed alongside the ship, the dead whale – which obligingly floated – was flensed of its blubber and the unmarketable carcase abandoned.

Once aboard, the blubber had to be chopped into pieces small enough to go through the bung of a cask, for the oil was only boiled out in port. The rest of the whale was valueless except for its 'whalebone', the baleen plates (essentially the same material as horn, hoof and fingernail) in the whale's mouth. Whalebone was for centuries the most effective stiffening material used in women's corsetry, while the oil made soap or fuelled street lamps; only later in the Industrial Revolution was it actually used as a machine lubricant.

A whaling voyage ideally lasted until all the blubber casks aboard were filled, with the first 'full ship' sometimes back in Shetland by the end of June. By late August, the onset of the winter ice forced all ships to retreat homewards, full or not. As whale stocks declined through unregulated effort, the 'full ship' became a rarity and often the cargo was augmented with other marketable products including seals, walruses and even polar bears.

For a young fit Shetlander it was a reasonable living; seasonal, with every expectation

44

Hull whalers around 1775.

of good reward – cash in his hand when Lerwick was reached, and often a bonus later, after the oil was sold. There were risks, of course. The commonest hazard was shipwreck, either through collision with an ice-floe or the ship being squeezed and crushed in the pack ice. A lesser hazard was being frozen into the ice late in the season, more common in the 19th century as declining whale stocks led whalers further north into Baffin Bay.

* * *

We have seen how in the first half of the century Shetland ship-owners emerged outside of the merchant-laird circle. Although hampered by wars, the local trading fleet continued to expand in the second half, as a new set of merchant ship-owners, mostly based in Lerwick, came to the fore. They developed agencies, handling exports to new markets on behalf of producers, and as trade increased, the port of Lerwick became a significant focus for both imports and exports.

Thomas Gifford of Busta owned the *Sibella* between 1740 and 1754, commanded most of this time by William Farquhar to whom the route to Hamburg, Bergen, Lisbon or Leith would have been as familiar as the passage up St Magnus Bay to Hillswick or Busta Voe. The lairds of Symbister were ship-owners and traders, with a succession of sloops named *Betsey* after the daughter of John Bruce Stewart. The first was a sloop of 65 tons, built in Leith in 1772. Commanded by Magnus Tulloch, she sailed for Hamburg in September 1781 along with the *Ranger*, the *Jeany* and the *Mary*. Laid up for the winter when the Elbe froze, she was damaged by ice and lost. The second *Betsey* came in 1787 only to be wrecked on Linga the following year. The third *Betsey* had better luck and a longer career.

45

Lerwick merchants prospered from their agency services to both whaling ships and the men they recruited in the port, along with the shipping of dried fish for lairds, or London merchants, or on their own account. By 1800, the Lerwick trading fleet had grown to 17 ships with a total tonnage of 552. Oatmeal from Orkney and salt from England or Spain were major import cargoes, although as fish exports – saithe and tusk especially – to Scottish east coast ports increased, more meal was imported from this area at Orkney's expense. Between 300 and 600 tons came north annually, to make up the perpetual shortfall in local grain production.

Although maritime technology was advancing, there was little change in the life of an 18th-century seafarer compared to his predecessor the century before. Charts of Shetland were more common, although their accuracy left much to be desired and the exact position of the isles remained inaccurate for many years. The best chart was actually compiled by John Bruce of Symbister, and published in Holland in 1745. Navigation was still an imprecise business; although latitude was relatively easy to measure, calculation of longitude remained virtually impossible. English clockmaker John Harrison eventually perfected the chronometer, which kept time at sea accurately enough to ascertain longitude, although it was not in general use until the 1800s. Aids to coastal navigation were practically non-existent.

Risks apart, even an ordinary voyage was an incredibly slow affair by today's standards. A sloop that could make eight knots in a favourable wind would be regarded as a 'flier', yet while tacking into a head wind the same ship would do well to gain more than three miles an hour to windward. It was usual to delay the start of a voyage until the wind direction was favourable, and in bad weather sheltered anchorage was usually sought, for progress to windward was virtually impossible. It was not uncommon for a voyage from Lerwick around to Scalloway to take a fortnight or more in adverse winds. Weather also delayed the loading of dried fish, which had to be kept dry; during a rainy hairst, a cargo might take a month to load. In ideal conditions – not often the case – Lerwick might be reached from Bergen in 30 hours, or from Leith in 48. More usually, a ship-owner sending his vessel on a trading voyage, say, from Hillswick to Hamburg and Bergen, would not expect to see his ship back home inside of three months.

Passage to and from Shetland before 1758 was a matter of 'hitching a lift' on any vessel available. In that year the first regular shipping service to Shetland began when the Post Office established a mail contract to provide six return voyages annually from Leith to Lerwick – a single sailing every month in alternate directions. Small sloops were used – fast sailers in good conditions but liable to frequent delays in winter, not to mention the ever-present risk of shipwreck. In 1776, John Mill, minister of Dunrossness, recorded "… in November we had accounts of a vessel that went from this countrey, Captain Bunthorne from Leith Commander, having on board Mr. McPherson a Merchant with his wife and two children; also Mr. Matthias Lyons a Merchant in Lerwick, who left behind a wife and 11 children; that she was wrecked on the coast of Bremen, and all on board perished…"

A typical mail packet of the late 1700s.

Another use for small fast sloops was in smuggling – moving goods without paying duty thereon. For many years this was a minor activity in the course of normal trading voyages – the odd package of tobacco, a keg or two of gin – but the business flourished from the 1760s. First the lairds, then the merchants became deeply involved in importing tea, tobacco and gin from Holland, or even timber from Norway. With fair winds, a sloop could clear Customs for Norway but make a dash to Holland, bring a cargo of gin and tobacco back to Foula or Unst perhaps, then speed off again to Norway for the legitimate timber cargo. It was easy to explain that contrary winds had made the voyage longer than usual. The sloop *King of Prussia* belonged jointly to Robert Hunter of Lunna, John Bruce of Sumburgh and William Bruce of Symbister. In September 1769, a Custom House log recorded: "Came in here and anchored the 'King of Prussia', sloop, in ballast which could not have by the appearance of it been in twelve hours, being all large stones quite wet and the grass upon them still draining and supposed to have landed her cargo of prohibited goods this night from Hambro on some part of Bressay or Noss as the ballast plainly shews it was taken in there…"

* * *

Europe-wide, all seafaring in the latter half of the 18th century was affected by wars which hampered trade and put large numbers of Shetland men – many unwillingly – into the British navy. Although powers of impressment had been maintained since 1631, the earliest record of a Shetlander impressed into the navy against his will comes during the Seven Years War. Delting Kirk Session, recording the death in 1760 of Thomas Clark, a sailor aboard HMS *Lenax* at Manila, noted also that he had been impressed in 1758.

This war was a struggle for empire, whereby Britain gained possession of Canada and supremacy in India. The British navy was expanded to sustain a conflict largely fought on opposite sides of the earth; when peace came in 1763, it's said that 900 Shetlanders were paid off from naval service. Not all of these had been impressed, for in 1774 it was stated that since 1754 an average of 100 men had gone into the navy or the merchant service every year. The pay in both was better than in the whaling trade, whose main attraction for Shetlanders was convenience and seasonality.

Whenever there was a war on, the seas round the isles became a hunting ground for privateers. These were privately-owned warships, licensed by governments to capture enemy merchant vessels, their owners and crews being remunerated through the sale of prizes. One defence against privateers was the convoy system, whereby merchant ships on busier trade routes were escorted in groups by naval vessels. Most of the naval activity of the Seven Years War in Shetland waters was concerned with the protection of convoys.

There is an interesting tale of a French naval officer – François Thurot – commander of a 44-gun frigate, *Maréchal de Belleisle*, in northern waters. In October 1757, his ship, dismasted in bad weather, was towed into Vidlin by local boats. Thurot wrote to John Bruce Stewart in Symbister: "Sir, I have occasion for some beeves, sheep, bread, meal and other trifles which I shall be obliged to you and your people to supply me with. I shall pay you the price you shall expect, but if you refuse, you can't take it ill that I furnish my self according to the rules of war. I am in hopes of your friendly complyance and assistance…" Faced with this polite menace, Bruce Stewart had no choice but to cooperate with his country's enemy; Thurot got his provisions and sailed his jury-rigged ship off to neutral Norway for a refit, after paying his reluctant supplier with promissory notes which were never honoured.

Britain and her colonists in America went to war from 1775 to 1783, when Britain admitted defeat and let the United States enjoy its independence. During this conflict the French and Dutch joined in on the American side, raising old fears of Dutch naval aggression and prompting in 1781 the rebuilding, arming and garrisoning of Lerwick's fort, renamed Fort Charlotte in honour of the then Queen. One result was the first recorded import of a new commodity – coal for the garrison.

There was a widely believed tale of this war that the famous Scots-born sailor, John Paul Jones, a commander in the American navy, sailed towards Lerwick bent upon attack only to mistake the red petticoats of the local lasses watching from the shore below the Knab for red-coated soldiers, and hurriedly retreat. Intriguingly, there is an exactly contemporary tale from September 1779 of two Cunningsburgh men, Adamson and Smith by name, who were fishing off Mousa when invited to pilot a ship into Lerwick. The vessel turned out to be a French warship, bent on attacking Lerwick, but Adamson thwarted the plan by persuading the Frenchmen that there were three naval vessels at anchor there. The two men were kept aboard the ship along with 100 other prisoners,

Fred Irvine's depiction of John Paul Jones' retreat from Lerwick in 1779.

before enduring a sea battle off the English coast when after a struggle they took command of the ship. The prisoners sailed her to neutral Holland and freedom, from where the two Shetland men got home early in 1780.

Published records of Jones' campaign in British waters confirm that the nearest he personally came to Shetland was on 3rd September, 1778, when his four ships – all French in origin but newly transferred to the United States navy – passed west of Foula before turning south again. Among them was the 44-gun frigate *Alliance*, commanded by Captain Pierre Landais, a man described as "eccentric; mentally unstable". Landais abandoned the squadron the following day, rejoining it three weeks later prior to the famous battle off Scarborough in which Jones' *Bon Homme Richard* captured the British frigate *Serapis* of much greater power, although the *Bon Homme Richard* sank two days later. Her American crew took over the *Serapis* and sailed to neutral Holland with the rest of Jones' squadron and 500 British prisoners. Later Jones took command of the *Alliance* and eventually escaped to France in her.

The record thus shows some truth in the two tales, except that the ship approaching Lerwick was almost certainly the French frigate *Alliance*. She took no significant part in Jones' action with the *Serapis*, and her voyage to Holland was under French command but nevertheless when the story came out Shetlanders were impressed by Adamson's tale, and it's said his laird rewarded him with a piece of land "rent-free to him and his heirs for all time".

Although Britain recognised the United States of America in 1783, only a few years of peace were enjoyed before the French Revolution threw Europe into a ferment. The aggressive new Republic was soon bickering with neighbouring states and eventually drew Britain, Holland and Spain into a war in 1793. This essentially European conflict doubled the size of the British navy from its American War level, and the recruiting process began again. In 1801, Walter Scott, of Scottshall in Lerwick recorded: "Since war started in 1793 not less than 1,000 sailors from this country have enlisted aboard ships of war, and hundreds more are employed in the Greenland whale fishery." Scott was Sheriff Substitute of Shetland; a former lieutenant in the navy, he was now in charge of the 'rendezvous' in Lerwick where both volunteers and and press-ganged men were enlisted.

The war with the French Republic saw success at sea for Britain's navy, with its fleets victorious over the Spanish at Cape St Vincent, the Dutch at Camperdown and the French at the Nile. On land, the situation was more of a stalemate, and hostilities ended in October 1801 with the Peace of Amiens. Napoleon Bonaparte was in full control of France by this time; both sides spent the next 18 months reorganising in anticipation of resumed hostilities, and the ensuing Napoleonic Wars lasted from 1803 to 1815. This was the era of the press gang – with a vengeance.

Chapter 8

The "remorseless perseverance" of the Press Gang

FROM its earliest days the British navy suffered a chronic shortage of trained seamen in wartime. Warships were laid up in time of peace, with only a few men aboard; when war threatened there was a huge rush to man the fleet and get it to sea, ready for action. The shortage remained perpetually chronic, for impressment was never a complete answer.

There was significant turnover in naval manpower, as up to half of every warship's company might be replaced every year through sickness, injury or accident. For safety's sake, untrained landsmen could not be employed in significant numbers and royal marines, although specially trained for sea service, were not really mariners. The impress service of the navy perpetually sought seaman volunteers in seaports, and took seamen out of homeward-bound ships. Outbound ships' crews were supposed to be exempt, along with landsmen, ferrymen and fishermen. In emergencies a so-called 'hot press' could be ordered – when there were no exemptions for any mariner whatsoever. True totals for impressment are elusive because volunteers usually qualified for a cash bounty and an advance of wages, so many pressed men declared themselves volunteers to earn some compensation for loss of freedom.

In early 1777, a rumour swept Shetland that the navy, expanding to meet the entry of France and Holland into the American War, proposed to press every man in the isles. Naturally, there was widespread alarm, with men heading for the hills and coastal hidey-holes whenever a strange sail was sighted. The lairds, even more alarmed at this potential loss of manpower to the fisheries, came to a deal with Captain Napier, commander of the impress service in north-east Scotland, promising to 'supply' 100 fishermen; half right away and half when the Greenland ships returned. Napier demanded and obtained his 100 more or less immediately, with little impressment involved. Doubtless, the lairds had other means of coercion and sadly the rules of impressment and the quotas set for each area were soon generally ignored in these remote northern regions.

We have already met Walter Scott of Scottshall. Of him, Arthur Edmonston wrote "Between 1793 and 1801 Walter Scott enlisted 1,100 men for the navy, when the population did not exceed 22,000 souls. Now in 1809, upwards of 3,000 souls serve in the Navy, with 600 going to Greenland – and as those who engage for this voyage are

Admiral Duncan attacking the Dutch fleet at Camperdown in 1797.

conceived to be complete seamen, they are looked upon by the impress officers as fair game, and are hunted down with remorseless perseverence". In 1809, by Edmonston's figure for men serving, one Shetlander in three was at sea in any given year. Over the twelve years of war, it's reliably estimated that between 50 and 60 per cent of Shetland's adult male population had served in the navy at one time or another. The many tales of the press gang in Shetland survived because traumatic events are not easily forgotten. Most of them had unhappy endings, for few of the victims lived to return. Shetland became a society where legal abduction and kidnap were a major hazard to normal life, causing a whole male generation to virtually disappear. By way of a present-day perspective, population statistics reveal that in 2007 a total of 1,930 males aged between 15 and 29 were resident in Shetland. Today, their absence would be an utterly unimaginable loss to community life.

HMS *Carysfort*, a 28-gun frigate, arrived in Bressay Sound in April 1803; when war on France was declared a month later a 'hot press' was initiated. George Vernon Jackson, one of her midshipmen, wrote of his Shetland sojourn in old age: "From South Shields we went to Shetland... we carried off every able-bodied man we could lay our hands upon. I think the number we captured in Shetland alone amounted to 70 fine young fellows. When the ship was on the point of leaving, it was a melancholy sight; for boat-loads of women – wives, mothers and sisters – came alongside to take leave of their kidnapped relatives... I often repented having made a capture when I witnessed the misery it occasioned in homes hitherto happy and undisturbed... These were strange times when a youngster of my age could lay violent hands upon almost any man he came across and lead him into bondage; but such was the law..."

Carysfort left Shetland in June with her human haul, 60 of them already signed on her books to complete her complement of 295. She spent the rest of 1803 patrolling in the North Sea and Kattegat before being ordered to the West Indies in 1804. Not surprisingly, fever decimated her crew there, and 14 Shetlanders died, the youngest Robert Ninianson, aged 16, while one sailor, Magnus Robert Hughson, was drowned. The youngest captive, Peter Henderson, was only 15 when taken aboard.

Walter Scott's son Keith became his assistant, an avid pursuer of naval recruits. He was joined for some years by Lieutenant William Wilson, a brutal individual who led a gang of local ruffians in capturing sailors. Press-ganged men were held in prison until they could be shipped to Leith along with the volunteers, and thence to one of the big naval bases on the south coast such as Chatham or Devonport.

Apart perhaps from a few Greenland hands most of these recruits would never have been out of sight of their home coast before, so their new world must have seemed utterly alien and fearsome in its vast strangeness. Close confinement, strict discipline and instant obedience were now their lot – all of it to be endured indefinitely. The navy wanted its seamen young, and preferably single. Once allocated to a specific ship and formally entered in her muster roll as a member of the crew, a man was 'rated' according to his previous experience: 'landsman' was the lowest rate, then ordinary seaman, then able seaman; the first two rates aged between 16 and 20, able seamen from 21 to 25. Boys under 16 were 'servants'.

By shore standards of the time, naval pay was good in theory. An able seaman's wage in 1800 was 29/6d – £1.47½p – per month of 28 days, a landsman's 21/6d. A sailor on a whaleship earned a little more than this, while back home, a man could expect to earn about 32/- for a three-month season at the haaf fishing. In law, pay for the crew was only due when a ship was decommissioned but in practice the men were paid two months' wages every six months with the balance due on decommissioning. While men could make arrangements for money to be remitted to family at home, this was similarly intermittent. There was some prospect of extra reward, for 'prize money' was earned by the capture of an enemy ship. While naval service presented risks from action with enemy warships, merchant seafaring was similarly hazardous, with ever-present risk of capture by enemy warships or privateers. There was little to choose between either service in terms of navigation and pilotage skills; His Majesty's ships grounded on uncharted rocks, dragged anchors on to lee shores or simply filled with water and foundered in storms just as regularly as did merchant ships.

In reality, the biggest killers of men were disease and accident. Men fell from aloft or ruptured themselves from over-exertion, or simply died from exposure or exhaustion in bad weather. Caused by dietary vitamin C deficiency, scurvy was a killer on prolonged voyages. Sailors were rarely dry, for their only weather-resistant clothing was of canvas coated with tar – hence 'Jack Tars'. The cold, damp shipboard environment engendered bronchial ailments, rheumatics, arthritis; sanitation was rudimentary to the degree that dysentery and typhus were commonplace. For every man who died, probably two were discharged the service through injury or sickness, for chronic cases and disabled victims of enemy action or shipboard accident were of no further use to the service. In the Napoleonic wars the navy suffered a total of 103,600 casualties – dead and injured – of whom only 6,600 were through enemy action. "Foundering, wreck and fire" accounted for 12,700 more, while disease and accident caused the rest, more than 84,000.

On board ship, each rating was given an action station and placed in one of two 'watches' for the day-to-day working of the ship. One watch did a four-hour spell of duty on deck in turn, while the other rested below. Boys, landsmen and ordinary seamen worked on deck, pulling and hauling under the officers' supervision, while the able seamen worked aloft, the youngest highest. Older, more experienced seamen worked forward, handling the headsails and the anchors. The wind only propelled a sailing ship after its sails were hoisted and set; human muscle power did this and everything else aboard, assisted only by block and tackle, capstan, hand-windlass and pump wheel. A naval vessel existed mainly to carry guns and use them, for which large numbers of men were essential. A gun was classed by the weight of its solid iron shot, from 3lbs up to 32lbs (17kg). A 24-pounder, the commonest gun in larger ships, needed a crew of six men to work it efficiently. These large warships, deemed fit to sail in the "line of battle" (hence ultimately battleships), mounted between 74 and 120 guns on two or three decks, were over 170 feet (52 metres) in length and displaced around 2,000 tons. Manned by a crew of 600 to 800, they were the largest and most complex machines so far created by man. Frigates, carrying 28 to 44 guns on a single deck, needed between 200 and 250 men, while even a small 18-gun sloop mounting nine-pounders needed 110 men. The officers lived aft below the quarterdeck while the men lived and slept on the gundecks in hammocks hung overhead, and ate at mess tables placed between the guns. Hammock hooks were placed at 14-inch intervals, although at sea with half the crew on watch, an off-duty sailor had the luxury of 28 inches' width in which to sleep.

By the standards of the age, food in the navy was plentiful and of reasonable quality compared to most workers' diets ashore, although their meat was usually salted and water was seldom fresh. Every day, a man was allowed a pound (453g) of bread, usually in the form of hard biscuit, and a gallon (this was a 'wine measure' gallon equal to four-fifths of an Imperial gallon; six pints or about 3.5 litres) of beer. Two days a week he received two pounds of beef, two days one pound of pork. On three meatless days the issue was one pint of oatmeal (for porridge!), 2 oz. butter and 4 oz. cheese. Four days a week he got half a pound of dried peas to make soup. Contrary to legend, rum was not official issue in Nelson's time, and it was issued only after the beer ran out. 'Grog' was issued twice daily, each man receiving a quarter-pint of 100°-proof rum watered down with three-quarters a pint of water. Allowing for wine measure it equates to 113ml of spirit, equivalent to four-and-a-half pub measures today. With alcohol available to that extent, it's no surprise to learn that alcoholism was another of the many hazards of naval service.

Probably the main factor that won Britain's navy its supremacy in the Napoleonic wars was a high standard of gun drill. In action this produced a high rate of fire; one

French privateer attacking British Indiaman in 1804.

broadside every two minutes was reckoned very good and, moreover, crews were able to sustain this rate of fire for long periods – long enough to overwhelm an enemy to the point of surrender. That said, there were far more duels between two ships than battles between fleets, while some officers went through 20 years of war without seeing a shot fired in anger.

Such was the service our 3,000 Shetlanders found themselves a part of, bound to it as long as hostilities lasted, with no hope of discharge unscathed. In those days a discharged seaman was literally abandoned at the dockyard gates, with money in his hand sure enough, but totally on his own as far as returning home was concerned. For chronic invalids or amputees, the long journey home was often beyond their powers. Most sailors were illiterate; only those who survived to reach home brought their stories with them. Naval records of the period – ship's logs, muster rolls, hospital records, and such – contain no more than basic information. We accordingly know more of officers' careers than men, for they could at least write a letter home, and were even entitled to shore leave.

There were two kinds of naval officers, one with a warrant from the Navy Board, the other with a commission from the king. Warrant officers had a particular vocation essential to the operation of the ship, such as gunner, carpenter, sail-maker or boatswain – usually promoted from the lower deck as they gained experience. Other warrant officers included purser, surgeon and 'master' – the warrant officer in charge of her safe navigation, answerable only to her commanding officer. Potential commissioned officers joined the navy as captain's 'servants' . Most of these became midshipmen in time and eventually lieutenants, while others were employed as clerks – basically the captain's secretary dealing with all his official correspondence. Lieutenants managed the ship under its captain's supervision, and only a lucky few ever became captain.

Promotion from captain to Admiral was by seniority and even slower; although three Shetland natives reached that exalted rank all had been long retired from active service. Alexander Fraser, son of a Lerwick customs officer, joined the navy in 1760, aged 12, becoming midshipman in 1767 and promoted to lieutenant for good service in the American war. He served in frigates and ships of the line, at actions in South Africa, Gibraltar and the West Indies, and was posted captain in 1791, commanding frigates until yellow fever sent him home to recover. His last sea command was of a little fleet of frigates and sloops protecting trade in the Baltic. Fraser was promoted Rear Admiral in 1811 and Vice Admiral in 1819; on retirement, he lived at Sandlodge until his death in 1829. His son John was drowned as a lieutenant in 1812, when his ship foundered on passage to America. Another son, Thomas, lived to become Admiral in 1870. Henderson Bain, son of a Delting mason, joined the navy in 1793 aged 19; promoted lieutenant in 1800, he commanded small ships by 1811 and was made captain in 1813. Details of his service are scarce; retired in England, he was made Admiral in 1846 and died in 1862.

Shetland warrant officers were more numerous. Sons of lairds and other gentry made good pursers – the officers managing the supply of food, water, spirits, firewood, candles and clothing, and keeping account of everything. Arthur Gifford of Busta was one such; his sister married another navy purser, James Yorston, who was years later described as "banker in Lerwick". James and Robert Scott of Melby became naval surgeons, James serving in numerous ships from 1803, surviving action and shipwreck before joining the huge naval hospital at Haslar near Southampton. His nephew Robert joined the navy in 1833, retiring to Melby in 1869 after a distinguished career in naval surgery.

Possibly the most eminent Shetlander to serve in the Napoleonic wars was Arthur Anderson from Gremista, later co-founder of the P&O line and provider of what are now the Anderson High School and the Anderson Homes in Lerwick. His employer, Thomas Bolt, saved him from the press gang by guaranteeing Anderson would volunteer when he was older, which he did in 1808, aged 17. He joined HMS *Ardent*, of 64 guns, as a landsman, becoming midshipman in 1809. The ship was on convoy escort duty in the Baltic and North Sea until early 1810, when Anderson transferred to the 10-gun brig HMS *Bermuda* as captain's clerk. On this small ship he did a variety of duties such as writing up the ship's log, writing letters for illiterates, dealing with official returns and other correspondence. He acted as purser, ordering stores and accounting for them. Commission on tobacco sales and other tricks of the purser's trade could double his monthly wage of £2 18/6d. *Bermuda* spent the war patrolling the English Channel or escorting Baltic convoys. Arthur Anderson was discharged from the navy at the war's end in 1815; probably ambitious, he stayed in London rather than return home – and made his fortune, eventually.

Although nearly every sailor saw action at some time in his service, few ever fought in a battle between opposing fleets. The most famous of these is Admiral Nelson's famous victory over a combined French and Spanish fleet off Cape Trafalgar in 1805, which put an end to Napoleon's hopes of ever invading the British Isles. His surviving ships of the line were soon bottled up in their harbours by blockading British fleets, so the only strategic option remaining to the French navy was to deploy its smaller ships to disrupt British trade.

On the morning of 21st October, 1805, a British fleet of 27 ships of the line commanded by Vice-Admiral Horatio Nelson caught up with a combined fleet of 18 French and 15 Spanish ships crossing their path to leeward. Nelson formed his fleet into two columns, which smashed their way head-on into the line of enemy ships, creating a mêlée where superior British seamanship, discipline and gun drill wrought terrible havoc among the enemy, of which 19 had surrendered by the day's end. A gale sprang up and ultimately only four of the enemy prizes reached Gibraltar; the rest were sunk, wrecked, or recaptured by their crews. British casualties were light: out of 17,000 men in the fleet, 449 were killed and 1,241 wounded. Proportional to the number of Shetlanders in the navy, around 370 of them could have served at Trafalgar but no accurate record exists. There were four Shetlanders on Nelson's flagship, HMS *Victory*, that summer, but Peter Robertson died aboard in June. AB James Garrick from Sandsound and OS Laurence Hughson survived, but OS Arthur Irvine from Delting was killed. Garrick was one of the

Close action at Trafalgar in 1805. *Royal Sovereign* third from right.

ship's boatswains, and helped to carry the wounded Admiral Nelson below. In later life he used to say, "I stood where Nelson fell!" Jeremiah Hunter from Bressay and David Gray from Unst are reputed to have been aboard, although neither appears on the ship's Trafalgar muster roll.

Nelson's *Victory* led one British column into the enemy, while his second-in-command, Admiral Cuthbert Collingwood, led the other in *Royal Sovereign* – the first ship to break the enemy's line. Her sailing master was a Lerwegian, 35-year-old William Chalmers from Twageos, son of the Collector of Customs. In charge of navigation, Chalmers supervised the ship's course towards the enemy line, while John Sinclair – possibly a Burra man – was at the wheel. An hour into the ensuing action Chalmers was "almost cut in two by a cannon ball" while talking to Admiral Collingwood, who later wrote to his wife: "He laid his head on my shoulder and told me he was slain". John Sinclair survived to return home ten years later.

After Trafalgar there were no more battles between fleets, although the war dragged on for a decade before Napoleon abdicated in 1814. By this time the British navy was shrinking to a peacetime level and discharging many thousands of its seamen, some who had not been home for fifteen years or more. Nobody knows how many Shetlanders survived naval service, but one thing is certain; their seafaring experience was put to very good use in the years to come as Shetland's sea-based economy shook off the shackles of war and began to expand in new directions.

Chapter 9

Sixerns, Half-Deckers, Cod Smacks and Sailing Packets

NAPOLEON Bonaparte's dreams of empire finally ended in 1815 with his defeat at Waterloo, and peace came to Europe after 22 years of strife. In Shetland, the wars had disrupted every aspect of life on both land and sea, especially with the absence of so many able-bodied men on naval service. Impressment continued to the end of hostilities, while the depredations of enemy privateers in northern waters ceased only after Napoleon's first surrender in 1814. With peace, the British navy contracted rapidly and men by the thousand were discharged as ships decommissioned. Once their arrears of pay were settled the navy had no further responsibility for them. Shetland seamen came off worse than most, having to travel the length of the country from the southern naval bases to a Scottish port before finding a sea passage home. Those who did make it back, brought with them experience and skills in almost every aspect of seafaring imaginable. Some even managed to save pay and prize money, ready to invest for a peaceful future.

During wartime Shetland's lairds and merchants had carried on as best they could with the home fisheries, while the Greenland whale trade continued only on a small scale. Both trades seemed ripe for expansion after 1815, particularly when the trade in fish to Spain and Portugal opened up again. Britain's growth in mechanisation and productivity sought new outlets, while her newly gained empire included colonies whose settlement and exploitation were seen as long overdue. Fundamental to everything was the retention of sea power and the expansion of ocean transport, in which the growth of Britain's merchant shipping industry presented Shetland seafarers with new opportunities to use their abilities and hard-won skills as an alternative to the resurgent fisheries in home and distant waters.

By 1820, Shetland's open boat fisheries involved at least 500 boats of varying size based all round the isles, crewed by more than 2,000 men and boys. All year round, as weather and daylight permitted, eela boats fished inshore for line bait, fourerns fished grounds up to 20 miles offshore, while Ness and Fair Isle yoals sought saithe in the tide roosts. The far haaf fishery was wrought during May, June and July to benefit from reasonable weather and long daylight. By this period, the Northmavine stations were the main centres for this fishery for ling, up to 40 miles out along the deepening edge of the continental shelf where the fish were most prolific. Although boat imports from Norway had resumed after the wars, and would continue into the 1860s, local builders created a slightly bigger boat for the far haaf – the classic Shetland sixern. Imported boat 'kits' had been assembled and repaired for centuries so the skills were already there, possibly augmented through naval service.

With a single mast and sail – derived from her Scandinavian ancestry – the sixern was a supremely able craft for her purpose, although challenging to sail safely. Her hull of oak and larch was strong, but light enough to be hauled up a beach by six able men. The symmetrical square sail of Viking times had been supplanted by one with a higher peak and a tighter leading edge or luff for better performance to windward, although with a penalty in that, when tacking, the yard and sail had to be lowered, passed round the forward side of the mast, then hoisted again on the new tack. It was imperative to keep the sail to leeward of the mast otherwise the pressure of wind could not readily be eased and a capsize was probable, if not inevitable. For the same reason, halyards were never tied when the sail was up, and the sheet under the skipper's control was held only by a few turns at most, ready for instant release. It's fair to say that sudden storms apart, 'backfilling' leading to capsize was the commonest killer of haaf-men.

Risks notwithstanding, the open boat fishery was a superb training ground for boys starting out in a life of seafaring. They learnt on the job, gaining skills from men of vast experience who knew the ways of the sea and how to handle their capable yet vulnerable craft to make a reasonable living from inhospitable waters. From the stations of Papa Stour, Northmavine, North Yell, Unst, and down the east isles and coast as far as Sandwick, sixerns ventured up to 40 miles from land as weather allowed. Eighteen trips per season was average, 24 ideal; a total catch exceeding five tons of wet fish for the season was considered very good, earning a man £5 or more.

While a well-handled sixern could safely make shore in extreme storms, a crucial factor was the ability of its crew to endure prolonged exposure to the elements. This was cruelly demonstrated at midnight on 16th July, 1832, when a full-scale hailstorm sprang out of the north-north-west sky, heralding five days of screaming hurricane. A great westerly swell had forewarned fishermen on the west side, while the Yell boats had used all their bait and were lying inshore, but the hundred-odd sixerns from the east side of Shetland had no inkling of the storm's ferocity until it broke upon them to leeward of the isles. Their only hope of survival in such conditions was to make for the south end of Shetland, and many did so against incredible odds. In a storm of such length though, hypothermia and debilitation took their toll and boat after boat succumbed as its crew's strength failed. Fortunately, the Dutch herring fleet was also east of the isles riding out the storm, and a dozen sixern crews were saved by superb Dutch seamanship, while a couple more ended up aboard merchant ships. Five survivors of a Whalsay sixern taken aboard an American ship only got home – unheralded – the following Christmas day, having been landed in Philadelphia. The true tale of the skipper's pet dog, aware of their coming and on the beach to meet them, is the only happy ending to a grim saga that

Sixerns at Fethaland.

cast away 31 sixerns and claimed the lives of 105 men. This heavy blow was not the end of the haaf fishery however, for life had to go on; boats were replaced and new men recruited into the fleet.

Since the 1730s, it had been customary for many haaf crews, when the main season was over, to pack up the lines and take aboard a few herring drift nets for a month or so to catch the herring that for centuries had shoaled close inshore. Before 1819, only several hundred barrels of herring a year had been cured in Shetland, mostly by a few lairds, for national efforts to organise a bigger fishery, based on the Dutch model of busses curing at sea, had never succeeded. Eventually it was realised that with herring so prolific close to the Scottish coast the fish could be caught and brought ashore quickly for curing, by fleets of small handy inshore vessels. This trade soon flourished in the Forth and the Moray Firth as far up as Wick after the wars had ended.

The sixern, carrying only a dozen nets, was never an ideal craft for the job, so in 1819, a syndicate of merchants and lairds formed the Zetland Herring Fishing Company to buy and operate two boats of the type in common use along the Scottish coast – bigger and more suitable than a sixern. The *Experiment* and the *Hope* were delivered from their builder in Orkney in 1821, and two Fife skippers hired to operate them and train up local men. It took five years to achieve success, but expansion was rapid over the next decade. By 1839, there were around 300 of these 'half-deckers' in the fleet, many of them built in Shetland, the rest a mixture of types and rigs bought in from Scotland. The trade was seasonal and subordinate to the haaf fishery, but fairly profitable for the fishermen.

The half-decker was so-named because her hull was decked over from stem to mast, giving her crew an enclosed fo'c'sle in which to cook and take respite from the elements. From the mast aft she was completely open, with tafts and flooring instead of a deck. The Shetland-built boats were rigged fore-and-aft with a gaff mainsail, foresail and jib – superior to the Scottish lugger rig in Shetland's voes and sounds. With a crew of six men, and 25 nets, the half-decker was well suited for her task, albeit too big to be hauled up between fishing trips. Through the middle 1830s, cured herring exports varied between 20,000 and 40,000 barrels annually, then declined a little.

On the night of Tuesday, 9th September, 1840, "the severest September gale in living memory" caught most of the half-decker fleet lying to nets off Sumburgh. Five boats were lost with all hands – 30 men – while a dozen crews were rescued before their boats foundered. Boats were wrecked coming into harbour and many more torn from their moorings and cast ashore to be smashed to pieces. It was said that not a single net set that night was ever hauled; 30 boats were destroyed and scores of others severely damaged. On the credit side, the ability of a well-handled half-decker to survive in such seas was demonstrated by Ertie White of Nesting, skipper of the half-decker *Confidence*. Her crew bailed and pumped to keep her afloat and when the wind eased the mountains of Norway could be seen. At the skipper's insistence, they set sail for home, and eventually made landfall south of Lerwick, hungry and thirsty but alive. They arrived home in Nesting ten days after they had put to sea.

This disaster heralded a collapse of the trade, which took 40 years to recover. Along with several poor seasons at other fisheries and a decline in the West Indian market for late-cured herring (following the emancipation of slaves), credit for new boats and nets was not forthcoming; the herring fishery was left to the sixern fleet and most of the surviving half-deckers never went to sea again. The final nail in the coffin was the collapse in 1842 of the Shetland Bank and the bankruptcy of the firm of Hay and Ogilvy, a business that had hitherto been at the forefront of innovative trade for 20 years.

When William Hay went into partnership with his father-in-law Charles Ogilvy in 1822, all had begun promisingly. Hay, in particular, was keen to develop the great potential in the herring and cod fisheries which his father had long sought to establish, and soon a modest fleet of small decked sloops was bringing cod ashore from grounds mainly south and west of Foula. The firm's complex of dock, quays, stores and shipyard at Freefield was completed within a few years, and their fish-curing station at Blacksness, in Scalloway, around 1830. Hay was also an investor in the Zetland Herring Fishing Company of 1819, and the firm's own fleet of sixerns, half-deckers and cod sloops grew steadily through the 1830s. They cured cod, ling and herring at stations all round the isles, marketed the dried products and shipped them to buyers as far afield as Spain and Portugal. Their shipyard at Freefield turned out all kinds of craft, from little eela boats right up to the three-masted wooden barque *North Briton*, the largest vessel ever built in Shetland. In 1840, their two-masted schooner *Janet Hay*, of 108 tons, was launched; only 67 feet in registered length – perhaps 85 feet or so overall – she was to venture as far afield as the White Sea, the Mediterranean and the Davis Straits in her lifetime.

For the sailing fishermen of Shetland, the rise of the cod fishery signalled a fundamental change, for the vessels employed were basically the familiar trading sloops in a new role – completely decked over, fore-and-aft rigged, seaworthy and able to keep the sea for long periods. Compared to the open sixern or half-decker, a decked sloop was, by the standards of the times, streets ahead in habitability and comfort for her crew, and in contrast to the complex handling of long ground lines of the haaf fishery, cod fishing was a simple business. The fish were caught on handlines, whose sinker was fitted with a wire spreader to separate a pair of toams, each with a single baited hook. Once at the chosen fishing ground, the vessel was hove-to and allowed to drift slowly over the fishing ground while all hands drew fish as fast as they were able. In its earliest days, with the wars still in progress, the fishery was wrought fairly close inshore, with only modest success until, in 1817, a Weisdale skipper relocated a prolific cod bank south-west of Foula, setting off a rush to exploit this new resource.

By 1830, there were over 70 cod sloops, mostly owned by firms such as Hay and Ogilvy, Nicolson & Co. and Garriock & Co., although many a sloop belonged to a single owner – her skipper perhaps, or a Lerwick shopkeeper even. The fishing trips lasted up to several days with the catch simply gutted and stowed in the hold for curing ashore. Once the Shetland merchants had mastered the salt cures demanded by a Spanish market that had lost its taste for dried ling during the Napoleonic blockade, the future for the Shetland fisheries old and new seemed prosperous and fair.

Nature had a hand to play in the game, however. The whaling trade suffered a decline in whale oil prices in the late 1820s, with competition from cheaper oils for textile manufacture and the adoption of coal-gas street lighting reducing demand for whale oil. Disaster overtook the Greenland fleet in July 1830, when the ice moved south earlier than usual; out of 91 ships 19 were lost, 21 came home empty and most of the rest were damaged. At one stage, there were 1,000 whaling men camped out on the ice awaiting rescue; by great good luck all but a few were saved. On 4th April, 1832, the *Shannon* of Hull left Lerwick, her crew augmented by 20 Shetland men. Three weeks later, off Cape Farewell in Greenland, she collided with an iceberg. The flooded hull did not sink; drenched and frostbitten men clung to it for seven days until two Danish ships rescued 27 survivors, most of whom subsequently succumbed to gangrene. Of the Shetlanders, only three lived to return home. Successive seasons were little better, then in 1836 even worse was to come, for in September six ships were frozen into the ice for the winter, including the northmost ship, *Swan* of Hull. Careful management kept the crew healthy until scurvy broke out in March 1837. Nine of the Shetlanders in her crew died, including harpooner Peter Hunter from Bressay, reckoned to be the best Shetland fiddler of his day. By the time the ice let the *Swan* free in May, only four men were able to go on deck.

This climactic cooling spread to the European side of the Atlantic, bringing in the late 1830s a series of cold summers that gave disappointing catches in all fisheries, and poor harvests ashore. The gale of 1840 exacerbated the situation. It was the practice for merchants to advance credit to fishermen out of season – to be recouped from future earnings – but with less produce to market, Hay & Ogilvy began to suffer what we would today call cash flow problems. In May 1842, the Royal Bank of Scotland foreclosed and the firm, its partners, and their Shetland Bank were all declared bankrupt. For a time there was economic ruin and stagnation – a period described as the 'hungry forties' for Shetland's population of over 30,000 people. This is the era that ended with famine relief and public roads built by labour paid for in oatmeal; young men began to drift away in their hundreds, seeking a living in the merchant service or a new life altogether in the colonies. At least their seafaring skills were in demand, for Britain's merchant shipping fleet had been growing rapidly; by mid-century there were 3.6 million net tons of sailing ships – and 275,000 tons of steamships.

* * *

For travellers, passage between Shetland and Scotland became a little easier through the early 19th century, with sailing 'packets' such as the *Lerwick Packet* and the *Coldstream Packet* making around six return trips from Leith per year. Mail came monthly from Aberdeen by packet until 1812 when the Post Office reverted to sending mail from Leith by any vessel sailing the route. Through the 1820s, topsail schooners, such as the *Norna*, of 104 tons, and the *Magnus Troil*, of 134 tons, were introduced to serve regularly between Leith and ports of call all round the isles. In 1835, the Post Office re-established a regular service for mail and passengers between Lerwick and Peterhead, using Hay & Co's *Fidelity*, of 126 tons, contracted to sail continuously between the ports with no more than two days in port between passages. Steam propulsion made its first incursion to the isles with a fortnightly summer visit from the paddle steamer *Sovereign* from 1836, although for a year-round steam service Shetland had to wait until 1861.

Going to sea had been second nature to most Shetland men for centuries, but through the 19th century, growing knowledge of the wider world drew seafarers much further away from their home shores than before – wars excepted. For those with wife and family the seasonal fisheries were preferred, but long absences from home were no deterrent to young single men keen to see the world. Besides, the prospect of becoming a respected shipmaster was attractive to the slightly better-off sons – legitimate or otherwise – of Shetland gentry. This is the era of Captain John Clunies Ross, originally of Weisdale, who settled and claimed ownership of the Cocos Keeling Islands in the Indian Ocean, and of Captain Andrew Cheyne, mariner and trader in sandalwood in the Pacific Islands.

The stories of such men survive on record because they were written in ships' logs or letters, while those of seamen with less education tend simply to be passed on orally.

One prolific recorder of his sea career was William Henderson of Papa Stour, whose first ship was the packet *Sheridan*, from Liverpool to New York with 130 passengers in early 1837, a passage of 28 days. There he joined the *Ganges*, bound for Quebec to load timber, which took 55 days, and brought the cargo east to Liverpool in 43 days. A voyage to Brazil in the *Cobotia* – hindered by revolution there – took six months. After a spell home, he sailed as second mate on the ship *Charlotte* of Aberdeen, to Archangel with salt, and back to Belfast with timber, a voyage of five months.

After a winter in a coasting brig, he sailed as second mate of the *Garrow* to Rotterdam, then to Quebec for timber and back to Liverpool in November 1840. There he signed on a Pacific trader; astonishingly, two Shetland sailors met in the vastness of the Pacific when William Henderson and Captain Andrew Cheyne met in the Loyalty Islands, east of Queensland, in September 1842. A month later, William Henderson and the rest of his vessel's crew were massacred and eaten by natives. Cheyne later named a coral reef he discovered 'Henderson's Reef' in memory of his fellow isles-man; coincidentally, Cheyne himself was murdered by natives in 1866.

Thankfully, their fates were not typical. More typical, and indicative of the pull of the British merchant shipping industry, were Henderson's numerous meetings with

William Henderson's painting of the *Cobotia* and a Brazilian brig.

Shetlanders – and ships from Shetland – in every European port he visited. The merchant service took men from the isles to places all round the globe and many found life in these new lands a more attractive proposition than their foreseeable future back home.

Chapter 10

FROM 19TH CENTURY DISASTERS TO THE STEAM ERA

BY the year 1852, the pain and hardship Shetland had suffered over the preceding decade were beginning to ease. A new business, Hay & Company, had finally emerged from the wreckage of Hay & Ogilvy, and slowly but surely prospered. The Freefield properties, the fleet of cod sloops, and even the schooner *Janet Hay* all eventually came back to William Hay and his sons, who doggedly pursued the same opportunities in the same trades as before. Through the 1850s, the old markets for late herring were depressed, especially in the wake of the famine in Ireland. But the cod fisheries fared better, despite a scarcity of fish on the home grounds which, in 1846, actually took the *Janet Hay* west around Cape Farewell in Greenland, north up the Davis Straits to the Disko Bank, above the Arctic Circle, in search of cod – which turned out to be unsuitable for curing. For a vessel not a great deal bigger than the *Swan* (Shetland's restored herring drifter), this was an epic three-month voyage of around 3,000 miles.

There were prospects nearer home though, which took the sloops to Faroese waters, then Rockall and Iceland, where they found cod in abundance. For these distant grounds a better and bigger craft than the home-ground sloop was required, for the longer trips necessitated the splitting and salting of the catch onboard. One factor led to another; more crew were needed to fish, so more bait and provision storage had to be available and so forth; there were well over 100 of these able craft fishing out of Shetland by the 1860s. Hay & Company owned the biggest fleet, around a score of vessels; fish-curers such as Garriock & Co. of Skeld, Nicolson of Scalloway and Thomas M. Adie of Voe had perhaps half-a-dozen each, and a number of Lerwick merchants each owned as many. There were even two registered North Sea Fishing Companies, one prefixed Shetland, the other Zetland, with sizeable fleets, and a fair number of cod smacks owned by their skippers or crews. All of these larger craft were bought in from ports all round the British coast; former trawlers from Grimsby or Lowestoft, trading ketches from Leith, ex-revenue cutters, private yachts, lighthouse tenders; any ship big enough for the job would do, although obviously some were more suited than others. In the latter half of the century, steam was replacing sail in many trades – and powering the private yachts of rich men – so sailing ships were going cheap in many places.

The smaller and older cod sloops, among them craft built during the 1840s in such places as Delting, Scalloway, Skeld, and Walls, still worked the home grounds – able to pay their way with smaller catches – but the 'Faroe Fleet' went further afield for much longer, employing over 1,000 men in its heyday. After a winter lay-up, their season began usually in February with cleaning and painting ship, before loading for the spring voyage to the Faroe Bank – 30 or 40 tons of salt, barrels for liver, bags of horse mussels for bait, several tons of coal, fishing gear and fish handling gear, spare sails and cordage, along with provisions and water for 12 to 15 men for three months.

From a seafaring point of view, the Faroe fishing sent far more Shetland fishermen out of sight of land for much longer periods than hitherto, compared to the haaf or herring fishing trips which seldom lasted more than 48 hours. The cod smacks, many of them fine-lined ex-yachts, could be hard to handle in unskilled hands and navigational skills of a high order were essential to find the fishing grounds in the first place, work over the ground for perhaps several weeks out of sight of land, and find the home port safely.

The tools for navigation were all readily available by this time. There were reasonable charts, compass variation and deviation were well understood, and patent logs to record distance run by the ship were commonplace. Skippers carried and used sextants, only for measuring latitude because small ships never carried an accurate chronometer, essential for the calculation of longitude. Passage was made by sailing a known distance from a fixed point of departure on a known compass course, aided by soundings, which in the trade were always made with a baited spread for a lead. The cod frequented the shallower banks and the fishing was easier in depths under 60 fathoms – if only to reduce the human effort required to haul up a struggling pair of 30 or 40lb cod from the depths. Faroe was not hard to find from Shetland, and the spring trip usually began with a visit to Torshavn for supplies of tobacco and spirits. Taking a new departure from Faroe's bold coast, the bank was readily reached, as was Iceland. Rockall was perhaps more of a challenge, for the rock itself is no bigger than Lerwick Town Hall, visible from only some 10 miles. Again, a departure from Sumburgh took the ship passing in sight of Orkney, then Rona or the Butt of Lewis, before making good the course and distance to sight Rockall. The distances were considerable; from Sumburgh Head, Rockall lay 410 miles WSW, the Faroe Bank 230 miles WNW and the Vestmann Islands, off Iceland's south coast, bore 580 miles NWxW.

Once on the chosen ground, sails were secured, a big canvas drogue or sea-anchor streamed, and the smack allowed to drift broadside to leeward as all hands from skipper to cook lined the weather side to shoot their handlines and haul cod as fast as they were able, continuing without pause until it was time to get the catch below. All hands then turned to the process of gutting, splitting and washing fish, stowing them in the hold layered in salt. This went on as long as fish were found, and while a 'full ship' – all salt used up in curing – was achieved on occasion, 25,000 cod were reckoned to be a very good trip, equating roughly to 100 tons wet weight in the hold. Whatever the catch, the fleet returned home in mid-May and sailed after ten days' break to either the Faroe or

Rockall banks, fishing until mid-August before the final trip of the year – usually to Iceland waters – returning in October for lay-up. Some of the smacks were built with a well – a floodable compartment to hold live cod caught on the last voyage of the year then taken all the way to Grimsby to be sold very profitably as fresh fish. The hands were paid per score of cod caught – each man cutting off the barbel under the cod's chin as proof of catch – plus a share of the net profits of the voyage. Not every smack belonged to a fish-curing firm; those that did brought their loads of wet-salted cod back to the owners' home base for drying on nearby beaches, while the others delivered their cod wherever the buyer of the catch might be located.

The Faroe fishing was a hard business, with as many hazards and risks as any other engagement open to a Shetland seafarer of the Victorian era. Most of the trouble befalling the cod smacks occurred making port – usually through missing stays and grounding – while many craft were wrecked in fierce gales when moored alongside a jetty, or blown from their moorings and battered beyond repair on the nearby shore. There were terrible tragedies, too. The smack *Turquoise* disappeared on passage from Iceland in 1872, taking 12 men's lives – six from Burra, three from Quarff and one each from Quendale, Nesting and North Roe. Peter Garriock, Lerwick fish-curer and merchant, lost his smack *Medora* with all hands off Shetland the same year, and the *John Walker* of the Shetland Fishing Company was lost with all hands on the Faroe bank in 1877.

There was widespread grief and sorrow throughout Shetland in September 1878, when Joseph Leask's *Telegraph* disappeared with all hands on passage home from Iceland. Her loss was a tragedy doubled, for she had 22 men aboard. This came about because Peter Garriock's smack, *Gondola*, had been wrecked at Iceland on 7th September, her crew fortunately saved. Her skipper and mate remained ashore to see to the wreck, while the other 10 got aboard English smacks. Two men were landed in Orkney and the others were transferred to the *Telegraph*, which was ready to sail for home. She thus left Iceland on 14th September with her crew of 14 and eight passengers; she was sighted at sea the following day, then vanished without trace. Among those aboard were five Whiteness men and eight Whalsay men, the others from all round the isles from Unst to Dunrossness. Most of those lost were young, single men in their teens or twenties; only four were over 30 years of age but they were all married, leaving widows and 16 children.

Joseph Leask was not the most fortunate of owners, for only two years later his cutter *Spell* vanished near Rockall, with 14 men including four from Whiteness and three from Whalsay. She sailed from Whiteness on 7th April and was last seen on 26th May during a strong gale and a heavy swell; it seemed likely that she had been caught and overwhelmed by a breaking sea.

Such was the way of the cod fishery. Many of the smacks traded during the winter, carrying away the dried cod to markets and returning with a variety of cargoes; salt from Liverpool, coal from the Tyne, Welsh slates, building stone and even flagstones. The heyday of the trade ran for two decades from around 1870, with the record catch coming in 1886, when Adie's schooner *Benito* delivered four full cargoes of cod from Rockall in 15 weeks and even Hay & Company's trading schooners, *Ariel* and *Columbine*, were sent fishing to Rockall. In 1889, skipper John Johnson, of Garriock's *Clipper*, hauled seaward to ride out a late Icelandic gale and when it abated after several days he found large cod abundant in only 30 fathoms, a hugely prolific new ground, named 'Hegli's Bank' from the nickname of its discoverer. This proved to be something of a swansong for the fishery, however, for its decline was not far away.

* * *

The Arctic whaling, the other distant water fishery for Shetlanders, continued its slow decline in the early 1850s as cheaper lubricants and illuminants competed in its market. Although between 500 and 700 Shetlanders still went to the Arctic every season, the surviving whale stocks were by this time far north up the Davis Straits and in reality their profitable exploitation was almost beyond the ice-negotiating abilities of purely sail-powered ships. To enter or leave this 'north water' ships had to navigate a belt of pack ice that opened and closed almost at random. The season of open water – and consequently the time available to catch whales – was short; for many whaling crews the temptation to linger proved fatal when ships were unable to sail out of the pack ice. This was how the Hull whaler *Diana* came to be ice-bound in 1866. She was a three-masted ship with an auxiliary steam engine of only 30hp, with 25 Shetlanders in her crew of 51 under Captain John Gravill. The fleet gave up whaling on 1st August and all escaped south on the 18th save the *Intrepid* and the *Diana*. The two ships lost contact and when the *Intrepid* escaped on 1st September it was thought the *Diana* was ahead of her – but not so. She became iced-in on 23rd September and thus immobilised for the winter. Malnutrition gave rise eventually to scurvy; Captain Gravill died at Christmas, and the first of her Shetlanders died on 13th February. It was 17th March, 1867, before *Diana* was free of the ice, when only a handful of men remained fit to sail her homewards. By the time she was brought to anchor in Ronas Voe on 4th April, seven more Shetlanders were dead, two of them that very day. Alexander Robertson reached home in Nesting, but died on 6th April. The fountain donated to remember this melancholy event still stands on Victoria Pier.

Such setbacks hastened the demise of the sailing whalers, including the remarkable *Truelove* of Hull, a three-masted wooden ship of 100 feet and 400 tons. She was built at Philadelphia in 1744 and taken prize during the American War of Independence in the 1770s; strengthened for Arctic service, she was a whaler from 1784 to 1868. Generations of Shetlanders served in her over these 84 years and amazingly she was not broken up until 1888.

The development of the jute industry in Dundee created a significant local market for whale oil, which was superior to all others for dressing jute prior to spinning. In response, the first of Dundee's auxiliary whalers were launched, massively built ships strengthened for ice navigation with a steam engine driving a propeller to augment the three-masted barque rig. By 1881, the British whaling fleet was reduced to 20 ships

The *Truelove*, built in 1744 and broken up in 1888, was a whaler for 84 years.

based only in Dundee and Peterhead, 19 of them with auxiliary steam engines. The last whale ship was built in 1884.

The power and capability of these ships was such that two voyages a season were usual; the first purely in search of seals for their skins and oil, followed by a whaling voyage proper in the later part of the season. As the century neared its end whales were extremely scarce, and most of the revenue came from the hunting of seals, walruses and polar bears. The last Shetlander to die in the Arctic was Robert Peterson from Lunnasting, crewman on the *Esquimeaux* of Dundee, in 1890, who slipped off a plank between ship and ice floe when sealing off Labrador and drowned before he could be rescued.

* * *

Nearer home, the Shetland haaf fishery also entered into slow decline through the second half of the 19th century. The markets for dried ling were maintained until the 1880s but competition from foreign producers and rising demand for fresh fish made the product harder to market. Maritime technology was improving, with decked boats and eventually steam trawlers appearing in Shetland waters to work the grounds more efficiently and safely. Most of the haaf men of this era were older married men, settled down after a youthful spell at the whaling or the merchant service, now content to earn a living nearer home. Although the greater inherent safety of operating decked vessels was recognised, the sixerns carried on at the haaf, and there was a rising trend of fish landings from open boats until 1882 – even despite the horror of the disastrous storm of 20th July, 1881, when 10 boats and 58 men altogether were lost. It was 1832 all over again, except the fleets from Northmavine and the north isles were caught at dayset, many miles off to the north and west. A sudden, unheralded hurricane from north-north-west, with snow and sleet, left the boats to run for harbour before the blast, towards a rock-bound lee shore in poor visibility in the darkest part of the summer night. It's not surprising that most of the lost boats encountered disaster in the tide-strings near the land, and six of the fleet of 26 working out of Gloup were lost, with 36 men who left 24 widows and 56 orphans. The east isles boats had to beat into the storm to regain the land and it's recorded that one Fetlar skipper, Thomas Tait, sailed his sixern, *Spray*, to windward more than 60 sea miles in thirteen hours to reach Bressay safely. Another sixern that ran safely before the storm into Ronas Voe is recorded as having covered 37 sea miles in four hours, an average speed of 9¼ knots. Literally, this 30ft boat had to be planing like a dinghy all the way. Haroldswick, Ollaberry and Mossbank each lost a sixern and her crew, while the loss of three men in a fourern from South Havera was a terrible blow to such a small, close-knit community. In the *Shetland Times* of 23rd July, the editor commented: "After thinking of the fearful loss of life and consequent suffering, the next question that arises is how long men are going to continue risking their lives in these frail skiffs. All round the coast on Wednesday night numbers of large decked boats were at the herring fishing, but they all arrived safely to the shore without damage to hull or rigging. We trust this disaster will do good in the way of utterly discouraging the deep sea fishing in sixerns".

The editor's words were prescient, although it took another quarter-century before the last haaf sixern was finally hauled up for good. The disaster did nothing to stem the decline in haaf fishing, obviously, and many men began to seek a less hazardous means of making a living.

* * *

It's believed that the first steamship ever to reach Shetland, probably a paddle tug, arrived in 1832 to tow south a dismasted brig that had been brought into Scalloway by a Hull whaler. Although steam began slowly to supplant sail from that day onwards, the transition took almost a century to complete. In 1836, the paddle steamer *Sovereign* began a fortnightly summer-only service between Granton, Aberdeen, Wick, Kirkwall and Lerwick, attracting passengers away from the regular sailing packets. For many travellers heading south, however, the port of Leith was favoured over Granton or Aberdeen and the sailing packet remained the conveyance of choice for a long time after 1836; while the passage might take a week or more, it could also be done in under 48 hours with favourable winds. It wasn't until 1862 that Shetland gained a weekly year-round steamer service, and as far as the movement of freight was concerned the steamers' cargo capacity was limited especially in the early days, so most of Shetland's exports and imports were carried by sailing vessels until the end of the century.

The 'coasting trade' between Shetland and the outside world was thus a very significant addition to the numerous options open to a local seafarer seeking new horizons. Cream of the trade were the regular packets, fast topsail schooners mainly, needing big crews of skilled men to handle them safely and make rapid passages. The schooner *Magnus Troil* served Shetland from 1833 until 1847, when she was replaced by the new topsail schooner *Matchless*, of 107 tons, from the yard of Alexander Hall in Aberdeen. This builder, hailed for his design of fast ocean-going 'clipper' ships, produced in the *Matchless* a miniature clipper of great speed and windward ability for her size that competed successfully with the steamers until 1881.

In Shetland waters, all movement of people and goods between the islands was under sail until 1869, when the little steamer *Chieftain's Bride* came to serve the north isles. Hay & Company had the ketch *Aspara* serving the north isles until 1890, and the cutter *Nelson* serving Dunrossness until she was replaced by the cutter *Columbine* – of Betty Mouat fame – owned by John Bruce of Sumburgh, in 1877.

The packet schooner *Magnus Troil*.

The clipper schooner _Matchless_.

Even after steam coasters first brought cargoes north in the 1880s, sail was the prime carrier of bulk freight up to the end of the 19th century. Most Shetland businesses were in the fishing or fish-curing trade, and either used their own craft to export each season's cured whitefish and herring, or chartered smacks from others. There were other exports – chrome ore from Unst, peats, kelp, even live cattle and oil from caaing whales. The islands' huge fleet of sailing craft needed skilled hands in carpenters' shops, smiddies, and sail lofts to fashion or repair hulls, spars, sails and rigging to keep the vessels running. There was therefore hardly a man in Shetland without experience of sail one way or another, and as the herring industry became paramount in home waters, and Britain's merchant sailing fleet turned to bigger ships of iron and steel construction, there was still a lot of seafaring in sail to come.

Chapter 11

THE HERRING BOOM AND THE RISE OF STEAM

FOR many years after 1845, Shetland's herring fishery was a small-scale affair of the autumn, undertaken after the end of the haaf season when the few surviving half-deckers and a small fleet of sixerns worked drift nets in August and early September. It was difficult to market the spent autumn herring, which did not cure well; full herring caught in midseason were worth much more, fresh or cured, but the haaf fishing took precedence.

Hay & Company had long sought to improve Shetland production of cured herring – only 1,100 barrels in 1874 from 50 boats – and had watched with envy as the Scottish herring fishery expanded in northern Scottish waters, using decked boats, fishing from June onwards and landing many thousands of crans ashore to curers at ports in Caithness and Orkney. Seeking to encourage local fishermen to adopt the same model, Hays made overtures in Orkney, guaranteeing to pay an attractive price for herring landed in June and July 1875. Ten boats from Holm and Burray came north and did well enough to encourage them back the following year, along with several more boats and one or two curers from Wick.

Around the same time, decked boats from Buckie and Fife arrived to fish long-lines on the haaf grounds. Shetland fishermen soon realised that the fully decked sailer of about 50 feet in length represented the way ahead for both line and herring fisheries, for such a craft could successfully work lines from March onwards, and carry a fleet of 50 herring nets through the summer season. Over a decade, the industry expanded at a remarkable rate, for the profits made allowed men to own their own boats and even re-invest in better ones; independent of the old landlord-tenant links, they could sell their fish wherever they pleased.

The first full-deckers were 40 feet of keel or more, clinker-built and straight-stemmed, single-masted with either a dipping lugsail or cutter rig of foresail and boomed mainsail. Below decks was a cabin with a cooking stove and bunks for the crew, a store for sails and gear, and a fish hold amidships. This hold was opened up for the herring fishery, but could be decked over leaving only a small access hatch for line fishing at stormier times of year. The first of these seaworthy and efficient vessels for a local owner, the lugger *Defiance*, arrived in April 1876 for George Irvine, a Lerwick baker whose brother became skipper. She was followed in May by the *Lass of Gowrie* for Burra owners, and the *Seagull* to Cunningsburgh. Others followed in droves thereafter; Hay & Company revived shipbuilding at Freefield while Laurence Goodlad's Malakoff yard and builders in Sandwick and Unst also responded to demand. Established fish-curers and ship-owners such as Hay & Company, Garriock, Adie, and Sandison in Unst all invested in boats, in either whole or part. Their return on capital came from the 'half-catch' accounting system whereby operating expenses were deducted from the boat's gross earnings and the balance divided equally between its crew and its owners. The crew's half was allocated among the men while the owners split the boat's share, net of expenses like hull repairs or replacement of sails and cordage. Crewmen might own the boat outright, or 'sleeping partners' ashore might have a share. In general, whatever the share structure, there was significant income for all. Notable in this respect was the 'Market Street Company', a group of six Lerwick seamen who invested their savings to buy the *Camperdown* – which cleared double her cost in her first season. By reinvesting their profits the six came eventually to own a fleet of three successful boats, and later each man built himself a new house out of the venture and "put a west side on Market Street".

By 1885, there were 319 'first-class' decked boats registered in Shetland, 43 of them in Lerwick. Whalsay, Burra, Yell, Sandwick and Cunningsburgh all had 15 or more, while every other parish and inhabited island had at least one – except Fair Isle and South Havera. This fleet was manned by nearly 2,000 men, many attracted back from the merchant service for the summer fishery. During the season, the local boats were joined by 450 Scottish and foreign craft and their catch of 370,000 barrels of cured herring set a record that was not beaten until 1900 – and never again by sailboats alone.

The hulls of these 50-footers were light enough to be hauled up by block and tackle and capstan, so they were laid up snug for the winter wherever there was a suitable shingly beach for the purpose. On the Scottish coast, the simple and cheap lugsail rig – with its massive unstayed mast hoisting a single loose-footed sail – was more common than the more complicated and expensive smack or cutter rig with foresail and boomed mainsail. However, the lug rig was less handy when negotiating Shetland's narrow voes and sounds, for the sail had to be lowered and shifted to the other side of the mast when tacking. At sea, this mattered less when drift net fishing but made the working of lines under sail impossible at times, so the smack rig found more favour in our northern waters.

In February, the smack-rigged boats were launched and rigged out for the spring line fishery beginning in March; equipped with maybe ten drift nets for bait and up to 12 miles of lines. They made two- or three-day trips to the haaf grounds, where their lines were shot out on a windward course with the smack close-hauled, and hauled before the wind with just enough sail up for the boat to keep pace with the line-hauling. On occasions, though, a shift of wind might leave the smack to leeward of her lines, and the only way to haul was by making short tacks to windward. Here, the handling attributes of the smack rig were essential, in combination with a skilled skipper and crew if the lines were to be recovered successfully.

This spring fishery prospered during the last two decades of the century, until the steam trawler had so reduced fish stocks on the old haaf grounds that line fishing was a waste of time. While it lasted, though, it kept the fleet busy until May, when the boats were rigged out for herring fishing – and the men cast their peats.

At the start of the season the boats fished on the west side of Shetland, landing in the 1880s to curers in Hamnavoe, Scalloway, Skeld, Walls, Papa Stour, West Burrafirth, Hamar Voe, Hillswick, Eshaness and Ronas Voe. As the summer progressed fishing effort moved clockwise around the coast, and landings followed; North Roe, Westsandwick, Cullivoe, Baltasound, Uyeasound, Mid Yell, Whalsay, Lerwick, Cunningsburgh, Sandwick, Voe, and Grutness. The fleet went to sea five times a week, shooting its nets nightly from Monday to Friday, hoping to land each night's catch to a shore curer every morning. There was a great deal of skill involved in the whole business, for the distance a sailing drifter could travel from port to fishing ground and back with her catch, inside say 18 hours, was entirely dependent upon the direction and strength of the wind. The

The heyday of the sail drifter, around 1900. The fleet leaves Lerwick on a calm evening.

best skippers were those who got it right most often, with ability to seek out a herring shoal within range, take a catch from it, and sail back quickly to a curing station. Many of the early-season stations on the West side were situated in voes or narrow inlets – Hamar Voe is a prime example – and they could be challenging to negotiate, especially in a slow-tacking lugger. At sea, exactly the right area of sail was used to shoot out the fleet of drift nets at the optimum speed, before sail was lowered to allow the smack to drift head to wind. It was customary to lower the mainmast to avoid strain on the gear; to safely lower – and raise again – a heavy spar 40 feet or more in length was an operation demanding a high level of seamanship and skilled coordination from all hands involved. That such skills were commonplace can be illustrated by the fact that, apart from the inevitable mishap and fatality now and then, only one decked boat – the *Alpha* of Burra Isle – was ever lost without trace. Over the winter of 1878, she had been converted from lugger to smack by Hay & Company at Freefield, and in April 1879 she sailed for Burra with six crew and three passengers aboard. The wind freshened to a gale overnight and the *Alpha* was never seen again. Many years later, pieces of her came up on long lines west of St Ninian's Isle.

The last clinker-built smack from Hay & Company's Freefield yard was the *Union*, for West Yell owners, in 1886, for more efficient designs of boat had evolved in Scotland. Carvel-planked over frames, the new boats were approaching 70 feet in length, carried more nets, and sailed faster with a two-masted rig. Their two favoured hull forms differed outwardly only in the shape of their sternposts; the 'Fifie' with very little rake from the vertical, the 'Zulu' with her aft stem at nearly 45°. There were still the two favoured rigs, the lugger now with mainsail and a smaller mizzen – as in the *Reaper* today – while the smack hoisted jib, foresail, mainsail and topsail on the mainmast, with a single lug-sail on her mizzen, similar to the rig of the *Swan* today.

The big new Scottish boats came to Shetland for the herring seasons of the mid-1890s. Local men admired them and soon began to invest in them, second-hand from Moray Firth owners. By 1900 ,the steam capstan was an essential feature in all the big boats; supplied by steam from a boiler in the cabin, its little engine made light work of working mast and sail and heaving in the mile of heavy bush rope to which the fleet of nets – "one for every foot of keel" – were attached. Not all the sail drifters were bought second-hand; many were built to order on the Moray Firth, where costs were lower. As the 19th century drew to its close, the Shetland herring fleet had 140 of these, fewer than before, but bigger and better. Hay & Company made a final effort in its building yard, and on 3rd May, 1900, launched the *Swan* from the Freefield boatshed which today, little changed, is part of Shetland Museum. At 67 feet, the *Swan* was the biggest fishing boat the yard ever built; rigged as a lugger at first, she became a smack in 1908. Although she was 'state of the art' in a Shetland context, her kind was already obsolescent, for 1900 also saw the arrival of the first Scottish steam drifter to fish in Shetland waters. For sail-powered fishing, the writing was well and truly on the wall, although 37 years were to pass before the last sail drifter finally gave up.

The *Swan* in her original lugger rig.

* * *

Every Shetlander at sea during the last half of the 19th century witnessed a slow but sure transition as sail-power gave way to steam. The wooden clippers that spanned the Atlantic, or brought emigrants by the thousand to Australia and New Zealand in the gold-rush years of the 1850s and 60s, gave way to ships of iron and then steel, themselves displaced in turn by steamers as steam propulsion for ocean-going ships became cost-effective and reliable. Gradually steamers gained most of the world's seaborne trade, especially after the opening of the Suez Canal in 1869. While Britain's merchant shipping fleet grew steadily to meet demand for the worldwide movement by sea of the nation's imports and exports, this growth came in steamships at the expense of sail. By the century's end, nine out of ten seamen were in steamers.

At home, the 19th century had seen a slackening of the landlords' dominance over the activities of their tenants, which gave the latter an element of financial and personal independence never enjoyed before. While seafaring of any kind was hazardous and hard by modern standards, for hundreds of ambitious and intelligent young men from the isles, a career progression through sixern, cod smack and Arctic whaler into the British 'deep-sea' mercantile marine represented an opportunity to use their abilities to earn higher reward through professional advancement. Travelling the globe brought them to new lands, and many sought a better quality of life thousands of miles from home while others settled in and around the seaports of Britain.

The Board of Trade laid controls on the shipping industry in 1850, including for the first time a requirement for ships' masters and officers to hold appropriate certificates of competence gained through examination after the candidate had spent a stipulated time at sea. The first step was second mate, for which a candidate had to have four years' total sea-time. Two years more were needed to sit the first mate's exams, and a further year for a master's certificate. Without this, a man could not aspire to command a ship "under God" and gain the coveted title of 'Captain'. So ingrained was seafaring in the Shetland character that along with seamen in their hundreds, the isles produced mate's and master's tickets and captains by the score. By virtue of their greater renown, the careers of Shetland captains, as with naval officers, are more widely known than those of seamen.

The best-known Shetland shipmaster of his era was John Gray, born at Valand, near Lund in Unst, in 1819. After haaf fishing in his teens, he made a Greenland voyage in 1838 before going south to sail out of Liverpool – the favoured port for the vast majority of Shetland seafarers at that time. He advanced to second mate, mate and then master of the ships *Sea King* and *Loodiana*. After a chance meeting with Captain Martin, his first captain and now master of the Gre*at Britain*, John Gray joined her as second mate. He was soon promoted mate, and then master of the ship when, in 1853, Captain Martin went ashore as marine superintendent for her owners, Gibbs Bright & Co. The *Great Britain*, a six-masted iron vessel of 3,500 tons with a steam engine driving a screw propeller, was designed by the great engineer, Isambard Kingdom Brunel, for transatlantic service and launched in 1843. Her first owners went bankrupt, then Gibbs Bright bought her to run to Australia. She was the finest ship afloat in her heyday, so to command her was a huge professional distinction for Captain Gray. Reducing her masts from six to three improved her performance and John Gray remained her master for 19 years, including charter voyages to the Crimea and India with troops. He often sailed with Shetlanders in his crew; first and second mates, Robert and Gilbert Peterson, in 1862, Peter Christie, third mate, in 1863 and John Angus, fourth mate, in 1864, while on one occasion he had four Shetland quartermasters – Gilbert Johnson, Thomas Scott, John Sinclair and William Slater. Captain Gray suffered from malaria, which possibly contributed to his disappearance from the ship early in a return voyage from Melbourne in November 1872. His command, recovered in 1970 from the Falkland Islands where she had been a hulk since 1886, is now fully restored and a major attraction in the port of Bristol where she was built.

The career of John Angus, a cousin of Captain Gray, was also tragically cut short. From Catfirth, he served two years in the *Great Britain* then sailed on the Australian coast. He was mate of the barque *Golden Age* when she was wrecked on Flinders Island, south of Tasmania, in 1872. He survived to command the coasting schooner *Corsair* but never fully recovered his health after the ordeal, and died in 1874, aged only 41.

In 1858, Brunel built his *Great Eastern*, a 700-foot iron monster of 18,000 gross tons, with both paddles and screw propeller in addition to six masts and 1.5 acres of sail.

Designed for service to the Far East, she bankrupted her first owners and was put on the transatlantic run. Magnus Manson from Bressay was in her crew when a heat exchanger inside one of her funnels burst, killing 12 men and blowing Magnus and several others overboard. Rescued, he returned to sailing ships, passed for master, and commanded two sailing ships before going 'into steam' for the remainder of his career.

Brunel's giant ship nearly drowned another Shetland shipmaster, Robert Sinclair from Dunrossness. Two days out of Liverpool bound for Quebec, his ship was run down and sunk by the *Great Eastern*; fortunately, all hands survived. Captain Sinclair later commanded ships for Nova Scotian owners, including the *Loodiana*, one of Captain John Gray's early commands. Captain Sinclair had left her when she took fire in mid-ocean; all hands perished including his brother Peter, and brother-in-law Arthur Smith, first mate and sail-maker respectively. He then bought his own ship, the *Larnica*, in which his wife sailed with him. He retired home after his health failed, and died in 1912.

By the 1890s, sailing ships had been relegated to the carriage of lower-value bulk cargoes such as grain, rice, coal, or timber. As cargoes lost value the need for speed diminished and the freight rates offered also reduced, dictating economy of scale and resulting in bigger ships with smaller crews – typically four-masted steel barques loading

Norwegian ships in Lerwick for examination during World War One; *Audny* **is a steel fullrigger, buil in 1882 as** *Hyderabad* **of Greenock. The iron barque** *Juno* **was built in Bremen in 1878 as** *Antares***.**

between 3,000 and 4,000 tons and sailed by a crew of around 25 men. Ships such as these needed seamen of great ability and experience to command them, as several Shetlanders did; men such as Captain Thomas Kay from Challister, Whalsay, who was master of the big barque *Earl of Dunmore* for 12 years in the Australian trade, and Captain Robert Coutts from Walls, master for 14 years of the four-master, *Alcedo*, of Liverpool.

It was customary in those days to augment a ship's crew by up to six teenage 'apprentices', trainee officers whose parents paid the ship-owner for the dubious privilege of learning the profession. Apprentices were generally treated more as very cheap labour than anything else during their four years of sea-time, needed before they could gain a second mate's certificate, but the system persisted because experience in sail was long considered by shipping companies to be essential background for officers in steamships.

Gilbert Harrison, later to be Lerwick harbourmaster for 24 years, was one of the few Shetlanders whose father – a prominent Lerwick fish-curer – could afford this career path. Aged 17, he was apprenticed to Milne & Co. of Aberdeen and joined their three-masted barque, *Inversnaid*, of 1,312 gross tons, at Cardiff in August 1896, bound for Colombo with coal. After 107 days at sea, it took six weeks to discharge the cargo and load ballast for Balasor in Bengal. In January 1897, rice was loaded for Madagascar where no cargo offered so a ballast passage was made to Newcastle NSW, Australia, arriving in July. Five weeks later a coal cargo for San Francisco was aboard, delivered after 71 days' passage. After eight weeks in port, *Inversnaid* left for Cape Town with grain, arriving just after Christmas. The year 1898 was taken up with a ballast passage to Newcastle NSW, a coal cargo to San Francisco again, and the loading of grain, this time for home. Falmouth was reached after 163 days, the ship towed to Cork in Ireland for discharge, and young Harrison reached Lerwick in May 1899, after two years and ten months away, and two circumnavigations of the globe.

He rejoined *Inversnaid* in Cardiff after only two weeks' leave for a passage to San Francisco with coal, followed by a grain cargo back to London. On 6th January, 1900, this cargo shifted in heavy seas and the ship was damaged, so seriously that she was put into Valparaiso for repairs which took nearly four months. *Inversnaid* arrived in London in September 1900 after a passage of 97 days. This completed Gilbert Harrison's four years of sea-time, whereupon he gained his second mate's certificate and spent the rest of his seagoing career in steamships. An era that had lasted 1,000 years was virtually at an end.

Chapter 12

THE LAST YEARS OF WORKING SAIL

AT the dawning of the 20th century it was apparent to most seafarers that the days of sail were numbered, except perhaps in the herring fishery, where steam had been a very recent innovation and both capital and running costs still favoured the sailboat.

The haaf fishery, producing salted, dried fish for export, was first to fall before the march of progress. Seafaring in open boats was not a favoured choice where there were more comfortable and safer alternatives and, by 1900, there were only four sixerns fishing from Fethaland. The very last haaf sixern, *Maggie*, owned and skippered by Charles Ratter of Setter, landed her final catch for curing there in 1903, when the station closed. He made a few more voyages for a year or two, as did a handful of large decked sixerns, fishing out of Voe, Dunrossness. The last survivor, the *Hope*, built at Freefield by Hay & Co, was sold to Whalsay in 1923, where she was lengthened and engined as a haddock line boat.

This haddock fishery had begun in the 1850s, gaining viability with the coming of steamer services, to ship fresh fish in ice to Scottish markets. It was a winter fishery, originally using open boats smaller than a sixern, working fairly close inshore. Ironically, men went to it while their decked boats were hauled up for the winter, and its risks were demonstrated in terrible fashion by the horror of Shetland's last two fishing disasters. First, there came a blizzard late on Friday, 9th December, 1887, catching Whalsay boats south of the isle – seven Whalsay men lost their lives that night, along with ten from other parts of Shetland. Then, a north-westerly hurricane broke upon the little fleet of boats from Delting, working their lines in the mouth of Yell Sound on 21st December, 1900. Four boats were lost with 22 men, leaving 15 widows and 61 other dependents.

Scots fishermen emigrating to Shetland from the Moray Firth brought their decked line boats with them, and their example was soon followed. In 1908, the first motor-powered haddock boat appeared; two years later there were ten in the fleet and the sailers rapidly faded away thereafter.

The cod smacks went the same way, slowly driven off the seas as the spread of steam trawling thinned out the cod shoals everywhere, and demand for dried, salt cod continued to fall, although the best quality dried cod still found ready markets in Spain at good prices. As time went on, crews became hard to recruit, as young men were more attracted to better incomes – and less arduous conditions in the herring fishing and the merchant marine. One by one the smack owners withdrew from the trade and their vessels were sold, often to Faroese owners. Adies of Voe ran the *Granville* and the *Seamew* into the new century, until the latter was wrecked in Hamar Voe in 1903. Nicolson & Co. of Scalloway ran their last smack, *William Martin*, from 1894 to 1906 when her master, Joseph Peterson, retired. She sailed another two seasons with a crew of Faroese before she was finally sold to new owners in Torshavn.

Sandisons of Unst, traders of every possible Unst commodity so long as viability lasted, also remained in the cod trade nearly to its end. They bought the former Hull sailing trawlers *Silver Lining* and *Thomas Henry* in 1895 and 1896 respectively, and ran them in the Faroe fishing for only a couple of years before more lucrative employment was found for them in general trading.

Hay & Company also held on into the 20th century – to the very end. They had bought their last smack, *Buttercup*, as late as 1896 and she was the last Shetland smack to fish the Faroe and Iceland banks with a wholly Shetland crew, in 1904. Sadly, her expenses exceeded her earnings. A Faroese crew went in her for another three seasons, landing their fish to Hays in Lerwick, but again the economics were against the venture. The *Buttercup* was then converted into a herring buss to fish and cure her catch aboard

William Martin, one of the last cod smacks.

at sea, which she did with moderate success until 1913. She was laid up all through the 1914-18 war and finally sold to Faroe.

* * *

The turn of the 19th century also heralded the dying years of the Arctic whale fishery, as whales became rarer and the demand for their oil reduced until its only outlet was among the jute-spinning mills of Dundee, where the last ships were based. They operated a two-voyage season to the end; in truth, most of their income came from the early voyage to the ice-fields off Labrador, for seals. The nine ships that went to the Arctic in 1907 were reckoned to have made a net loss of £50,000 among them, and only two ships carried on. The last whales were harpooned and killed in 1910, and when the last nine Shetlanders ever to ship for Greenland went out in the *Scotia* for the 1911 season, the catch consisted of seals, walrus and polar bears. The *Morning* and the *Balaena* went north for the last time in 1913 and returned with empty holds. The Dundee whale ship fleet was dispersed, some to Antarctic expeditions, others into service round Labrador and Hudson's Bay. By December 1915, only two – the *Active* and the *Morning Star* – remained in Dundee, laid up awaiting the scrapyard. The needs of war intervened and both were requisitioned and refitted to carry cargo. Grossly overloaded they sailed for Archangel, the *Active* under Captain William Leask from Sandsound, with second mate James Jamieson from Bigton. A day or so out of Dundee they were caught by a south-easterly hurricane and the old ship began to leak. Before she foundered somewhere north-east of Orkney, drowning all hands, James Jamieson found time to write a message to his family and seal it in a bottle which, remarkably, drifted ashore in Orkney and eventually reached its destination. The bodies of James Jamieson and one other crewman came ashore in Rousay, where they were buried.

Around the turn of the century, there were still 3,500 ocean-going sailing ships in commission, of which the British fleet of 800 was the largest by a good margin over Norway, whose ship-owners were buying British sailing tonnage as fast as it came on the market. More than 2,000 Shetland men were sailing deep-sea, most of them in steamships by now, making safer and more predictable voyages with their engagements seldom longer than two years. Younger men still shipped out in sail here and there, probably for the experience and adventure, while older shipmasters – rarely mates – were content to see out their careers commanding well-managed ships and barques out of Glasgow or Liverpool. The sea was never predictable, though, and there were times when skill and seamanship could not prevent hardship and disaster.

The four-masted Glasgow barque *Springbank* sailed from Hamburg in early June 1908, bound for Santa Rosalio in the Gulf of California with a cargo of coke and patent fuel. Well built, equipped and manned, although operated with strict economy at minimal cost, she had four Shetland seamen aboard – Nicky Tulloch from Cullivoe, Tom Irvine from Sellafirth, Laurence Tait from Aith and James Hardy from Mossbank – looking forward to a routine voyage of 120 days or so. It was soon found, however, that the light coke and the heavy briquettes had been stowed wrongly and the ship was out of trim. Sail had to be reduced in anything of a wind and tacking was nearly impossible. Consequently, it took 82 days to reach Cape Horn and another six weeks of tacking westward to get around the Cape in the strong gales and heavy seas that prevailed. It was impossible to cook food; with stores and water running low, the crew suffered terribly from both hunger and cold. An Orkney seaman and the captain's wife died before the ship was able to sail out of the bad weather. Wishing to bury her on land, the captain had his wife's coffin filled with flour and sealed with pitch and canvas to make it airtight. In warmer waters, the ship's bottom grew weeds, slowing her progress even further. Just when it seemed the coffin could stay aboard no longer, an uninhabited offshore island was reached where the captain was able to bury his wife. It took another month of beating against the wind up the Californian Gulf to reach port in late January 1909 – a passage of 210 days, or nearly seven months.

One of the last Shetland shipmasters to command an ocean-going square-rigger was Captain John Isbister of Strom, Whiteness, for he was master of the full-rigged three-master *Dalgonar* of Liverpool, in 1913. In an uneventful voyage, he took a cargo of coal out to Callao in Peru, and was fixed to load nitrate fertiliser at Taltal in Peru for Europe. This involved a ballast passage between the ports and the *Dalgonar* sailed from Callao on 14th September. The shingle ballast loaded in Callao was notorious for its tendency to shift in bad weather, even when securely boxed and shuttered in the hold – and its shore suppliers were notorious for giving short weight. About halfway to her destination, on 9th October a sudden squall laid the *Dalgonar* on her beam ends and the ballast shifted into the lee side of the hold. To right the ship quickly the masts were cut away, but the list hardly decreased so orders were given to lower a lifeboat. With ten men in it, the boat was caught and capsized among the tangle of spars and rigging alongside. Seven men made it back aboard; Captain Isbister, aged 61, went out along the stump of the mizzenmast to throw a rope to the three men in the water, but he was swept away by a wave and seen no more. The *Dalgonar* stayed afloat, and her survivors were rescued by a boat's crew from the French barque *Loire* on 19th October, while the derelict vessel drifted more than 5,000 miles across the Pacific before she finally wrecked herself on a coral reef.

Probably the last Shetlander to lose his life in a square-rigger was also one of the youngest, and his loss was all the more poignant because it happened virtually on his own doorstep, so to speak. The morning after a south-westerly gale in April 1915, quantities of floating wreckage were seen from Culswick, including a body, and although the sea was still heavy a boat was launched to recover it. To the astonishment of the Culswick men it was recognised as being that of Christopher Fraser of Scarpigarth, in Walls, a young man aged only 18 who had left home to go sailing the year before. He was in the Australian-registered barque *Avante Savoia*, bound from Iquique, in Chile, to Rotterdam with a cargo of nitrates. In the dark of the night the barque had struck the Stacks of Burgi, east of the entrance to Vaila Sound, and broken up; there were no survivors. It was thought that with a war taking place, the ship had taken the safer northern route to avoid the English Channel; more than likely the master's reckoning of her position was in error and the unexpected sighting of breaking sea on a barren cliff-girt coast left no time to alter course before she struck. Another nine bodies were later recovered, along with Christie Fraser's ditty-box – and the remains of his fiddle.

As British sailing ships became increasingly unprofitable to operate before the First World War, their numbers declined; their viability was made even worse after the Panama Canal was fully opened in 1916. Sailing ships were easy targets for enemy raiders and submarines in wartime, and no more than a handful survived in 1918. Indeed, by 1928 it was reckoned that there were no more than 100 square-riggers afloat in the world. In Shetland, there was a final postscript to deep-water sail in December 1920; an incident with a happy ending, where seamanship of the highest order saved a square-rigger from certain destruction.

During a south-easterly gale on the morning of 1st December, 1920, men at Skaw in Whalsay observed a large three-masted sailing ship labouring in the heavy seas between Whalsay and Skerries, flying signals of distress and being slowly carried into the bight formed by Whalsay, Yell and Fetlar. Five Skaw men launched a boat and successfully put two of them aboard – William Irvine who had been in square-riggers, and Laurence Hutchison for his knowledge of the area. Left in the small boat were John Bruce, Hugh Bruce and Laurence Bruce, who got ashore safely with the aid of a tow from a motor boat. The square-rigger turned out to be the *Marion Chilcott*, a Clyde-built three-master now owned in America and converted into one of the first true tankers, carrying her cargo in bulk tanks originally from America to Hawaii. She had sailed in ballast from Aalborg four days before, bound for the Caribbean to load another cargo of diesel oil for Europe. Her master was over 60, her officers and 24 crew mostly inexperienced; after Skerries

The *Marion Chilcott*, saved by five Skaw men in 1920.

87

Light and breakers were sighted, the ship was brought head to wind but heavy seas caused damage and swept away a lifeboat before she managed to reach clear water north-west of Skerries. With the Skaw men aboard sail was set again, and they successfully guided the *Marion Chilcott* into Mid Yell and brought her safely to anchor, where she lay for a month before a tug arrived with replacement gear and her voyage was resumed. What the folk of Mid Yell thought when a 300-foot square-rigger appeared out of the 'mirkening' on a winter's afternoon is not recorded, but the Whalsay men's deeds were acclaimed; each man received a gold medal from the US government, the bronze medal of the RNLI – and £13, his share of the pilotage fee of $200.

In the 20th century, Shetland's locally-owned sailing fleet carried on trading as long as its owners – mainly the larger herring-curing firms – could find men to crew them and paying cargoes to carry. The topsail schooner *Ariel*, built at Cowes in 1844, came to Shetland as a cod fisher in 1860 but spent many years carrying imports and exports, surviving fire and stranding in the process. She was last owned by J. W. Robertson, fish-curer and merchant, who had an engine installed in 1914. *Ariel* was sunk by a German submarine off Peterhead, in July 1917. Even older was the schooner *Columbine*, built at Cowes in 1834 and bought by Hay & Company in 1869. In her time she carried herring to Stettin, whale crangs to Montrose and kelp to Granton, bringing back timber from Norway, coals from Newcastle, wet cod from Buckie and Tromso, along with countless commodities for Hay's retail trade. She was retired in 1914, sold for £20 and broken up at Hoswick. Hay's got as much life out of their fleet as possible, for they also owned the 36-ton cutter-rigged sloop, *Spy*, built in 1838 and used mainly for fetching and carrying round the isles until sold to Faroe in 1902. In that year Lerwick fish-curer, boat-owner and blacksmith, John Brown, bought the three-masted barquentine *Linus*, a substantial vessel of 170 tons and ran her until war came in 1914. Of the Faroe smacks only Hay's *Buttercup* fished after 1909, while Sandison of Unst kept their ketch *Silver Lining* in trading until 1919.

Built in 1885 as a Hull trawler, the *Silver Lining* came to Unst in 1895 for the Faroe fishing. After two seasons she was kept trading all year round, all through the time of the herring boom when there was plenty of work, exporting cured herring to Hamburg or chromite to Liverpool and returning with coal, cement, and general cargo. When war broke out in 1914, Sandisons were allowed to keep her running under Admiralty direction, importing coal and exporting chromite. When the convoy system was introduced in 1917, sailing vessels were exempted for obvious reasons and allowed to sail on their own – subject to anchoring between sunset and sunrise. This was seldom feasible in practice, and one night in October 1916 the *Silver Lining*, sailing happily towards Fair Isle, was found and 'arrested' by a destroyer, which towed her ignominiously into Kirkwall where her skipper had to answer for his breach of regulations. For want of dry-docking during the war the *Silver Lining* was leaking badly by 1918 and was laid up until new Faroese owners took her away in 1919. Her departure seemed to signal the end of commercial sail in Shetland, but there was one more vessel to come.

The Lerwick barquetine *Linus*.

Without a ship after the *Ariel* was lost in 1917, J. W. Robertson bought an obsolescent three-masted schooner of 275 tons from Latvian owners in 1927. Built in 1908 to carry Baltic timber, she was renamed *Dorjoy* after J. W.'s daughters, Dorothy and Joyce. She had no engine, and therefore only hand winches for working anchors and cargo. Laid up in winter to save insurance costs, she sailed from April to September – usually in ballast south and returning loaded with coal, from Leith or Blyth. In April 1930, *Dorjoy* loaded at Skeld a cargo of telegraph poles salvaged out of the steamer *Ustetind*, wrecked at Silwick in December1929. Some of the poles were delivered to Scalloway for holding up the village's first street lamps, and the remainder taken south to Newcastle. The ship returned north in June with a cargo of coal from Blyth – the last ever voyage by a Shetland-owned

Dorjoy **at anchor in Skeld Voe.**

sail trader. Her master was Robert Roberts, a Welshman, and the Shetlanders in her crew were Magnus Malcolmson from Tingwall, Frank Cowie from Scalloway, Joseph Fraser from Reawick, and Andrew Ridland from Lerwick. The *Dorjoy* was subsequently moored off Gremista as a coal hulk until her coal cargo was sold off. Sometime in the mid-30s she ended up on the beach where she mouldered away over the years, parts of her still visible today.

After the *Swan* in 1900, only two more sailboats were built, both by Robert Jamieson at Sandsayre, in Sandwick. The *Comorin* of 1903 was the last, bigger than the *Swan*; her builder lived to see her broken up at Broonie's Taing 30 years later. The peak year for Shetland's herring boom came in 1905, when 1,783 boats landed 645,834 crans (110,210 tonnes) of herring. Of this fleet Shetland owned 378 sailboats, 281 exceeding 45 feet of keel. The combined area of the whole fleet's nets was bigger than Bressay, while the bush ropes, if tied end to end, would reach comfortably from Lerwick to New York. More significantly, there were 300 steam drifters present. The steamer could travel well offshore every night and catch next day's market whatever the wind, and the sailers found it hard to compete. Nearly 200 of them had gone by 1914, when the first motor boats appeared. The 1914-18 war took most of Shetland's fishermen into the Royal Navy,

Graveyard of sail: *Dorjoy* and two older hulks at Gremista.

The *Cormorin*, last and biggest of the Shetland-built sail drifters.

and many of the boats had to be laid up for lack of manpower. By 1920 the smaller line fishing boats were all motorised, and when the herring fishing got underway again there were 87 sailers, 12 steamers and 28 converted motor boats in the fleet. Powered by reliable Kelvin and Gardner paraffin engines, these ex-sailers were cheap to convert, economical to run and a better investment than a steam drifter, so year by year the sailers' numbers declined; they were scrapped or motorised. The *Swan* received her engine in 1936 – saving her for posterity – while only four sailers sought herring that year, the *Valkyrie* and the *Brothers Pride* of Whalsay, the *Flowing Stream* of Burra and the *Gracey Brown* of Lerwick. The latter sailed alone in 1937, but the shoals were only found 50 miles offshore or more and she earned a paltry £19 for her season before her owner and skipper Laurence Anderson put her up for sale. So ended 1,000 years of vocational seafaring under sail in Shetland.

It wasn't the end of sail, of course, for inbred habits die very hard. Recreational sail endures to this day, be it in Shetland models, dinghies or yachts, be it competitive or otherwise. Shetlanders are still crossing oceans under sail, and we're fortunate indeed to have the reincarnated *Swan* as a tangible reminder of an age passed but not forgotten. Scratch most of us Shetlanders, and salt water will still flow along with the blood.

The *Brothers Pride* lies alongside the *Maggie Peterson* in Lerwick small boat harbour, 1934.

Glossary

AB	Able Seaman
Baa	Shallow reef dangerous to ships
Blaand	Refreshing whey-based drink
Bower	Biggest anchor carried aboard a ship
Cran	Measure of herring – four baskets, or 37.5 gallons
Dayset	Dusk
Far Haaf	Line fishing grounds, up to 40 miles offshore
Hairst	Harvest time; autumn
Kabe	Thole pin
Matties	Early season herring, not full of roe
Meid	Transect formed by two shore features in line
Mirkening	Darkening
OS	Ordinary Seaman
Routh	Wooden pad on gunwale beneath oar
Smookie	Smock
Tafts	Thwarts
Toams	Traces

INDEX

General

People and persons

Vessels